YO-AQM-546

MONEY

How to Get It, Keep It, Make It Grow

By Tama McAleese

THE CAREER PRESS
180 FIFTH AVE.,
PO BOX 34
HAWTHORNE, NJ 07507
1-800-CAREER-1
201-427-0229 (OUTSIDE U.S.)
FAX: 201-427-2037

MONEY: HOW TO GET IT, KEEP IT, MAKE IT GROW

ISBN 1-56414-013-X, $9.95

Cover design by Harvey Kraft

Copies of this book may be ordered by mail or phone directly from the publisher. To order by mail, please include price as noted above, $2.50 handling per order, plus $1.00 for each book ordered. (New Jersey residents please add 7% sales tax.) Send to: The Career Press Inc., 180 Fifth Avenue., PO Box 34, Hawthorne, NJ 07507.

Or call Toll-Free 1-800-CAREER-1 to order using your VISA or Mastercard or for further information on all titles published or distributed by Career Press.

Attention: Schools, Organizations, Corporations

This book is available at quantity discounts for bulk purchases for educational, business or sales promotional use.
Please contact: Ms. Gretchen Fry,
Career Press,
180 Fifth Ave.,
Hawthorne, NJ 07507
or call 1-800-CAREER-1

Acknowledgements

To Jim

Who still loved me though I dedicated my first book—
Get Rich Slow—to my clients!

What to Do Before You Even Read This Book

1. Pay off *all* your credit card consumer debt. The most dangerous and destructive personal financial problem facing Americans today is "credit card crunch." I can promise you a *guaranteed,* **double digit** annual rate of return—simply pay off your credit card balances, slowly but surely.

2. Build an emergency or "rainy day" money fund. Stash some cash by "paying yourself first" in an interest-bearing checking, saving, or credit union account, which will keep it out of sight, take it out of your paycheck before you see it, or be systematically set up on an automatic payroll deduction. *If you don't actually receive the money, you won't be tempted to spend it.*

3. Sit down *tonight,* turn off the TV, and assemble a simple budget, together with your spouse and children, if possible. (My first book, **Get Rich Slow,** contains an easy-to-understand, step-by-step plan for figuring your budget.) Assign everyone some responsibility for making consistent progress.

   A budget does not *take* time; it **saves** time. It doesn't *prevent* you from having what you want; it **allows you to achieve** those financial rewards you're seeking. If you're planning your own financial revolution, you need a map to guide you: your budget.

4. Defer large purchases such as a new home or a car until you are sure you can *really* afford them, *even (especially) if your future financial life turns sour.*

5. Pay yourself first, but stop buying your children. Your child may *want* expensive designer jeans, but he or she certainly *needs* a college education or other vocational training more. Give your children the most valuable gifts of all—your time and love; *that* will cost you absolutely nothing.

Contents

Foreword   8

Chapter 1
Your Battle for Investment Survival   11

Chapter 2
Meet the Public's Financial Advisors   21

Chapter 3
Will the Real Financial Planners Please Stand Up?   31

Chapter 4
Your Financial Road Map   41

Chapter 5
Some Myths of Investing   47

Chapter 6
The Laws of Investing   57

Chapter 7
Teaching Your Child the Value of Money   71

Chapter 8
The Suddenly Single Investor   81

Chapter 9
Retirement Myths Can be Hazardous to Your Future Financial Health   93

Contents

Chapter 10
The Penthouse or the Poorhouse   99

Chapter 11
The Last Frontier: College Funding   113

Chapter 12
Where's *Your* Piggy Bank?   123

Chapter 13
Using Your Kids for a Change   137

Chapter 14
Short-Term Money   147

Chapter 15
Investing for the Long Haul   155

Chapter 16
How to (Not) Play the Market   173

Chapter 17
Mutual Fund-amentals   181

Chapter 18
Tangible Assets   201

Chapter 19
The Ways to the Means   219

Chapter 20
So Where *Do* Your Put Your Money?   231

Chapter 21
Special Strategies to Cover Your Ass-ets   243

Index   253

Foreword

If I were a baseball player, I'd probably never be the Home Run Queen. Solid base hits would be fine with me.

As a chef, I'd avoid risky souffles and sauces that separate. Give me a simple recipe I can't screw up.

And I would choose refueling a stunt plane on the ground over wing-walking 2,000 feet in the air *any*time.

All of which should tell you one thing about me: *I am risk adverse.*

Now that's not the same as "playing it safe." Even the simplest recipes sometimes don't work. And more people die in cars (on the ground) than in air accidents (up there) every year.

And that's the whole point—**There is no such *thing* as SAFE!** Not in life, and certainly not in the investment world. Creating wealth without inherent risks is *impossible!* There are *no* 30% CDs, *very few* (if any) penny stocks that will become the next IBMs, and *no* secret formulas you can afford that will guarantee hefty profits *and* no losses year after year.

Not that there aren't *scads* of people out there—many calling themselves "professionals" of one stripe or another—who promise exactly that...and more! These glad-handers are one of two types: (1) vested interests, and, perhaps even more dangerous, (2) well-meaning incompetents. The former will cost you money by design; the latter will lose it by accident. But the result will be the same: less money in your pocket, more in theirs.

Don't believe these salespeople. Because that's exactly what they are—people trying to *sell* you some product. For the most part, they do *not* have *your* best interests at heart. Though I guarantee they could tell you *their* commissions this month to the penny, without a moment's thought.

MONEY: *How to Get It, Keep It and Make It Grow* will teach you to separate the truth from the hype, the facts from the fiction. It will *not* give you a secret formula to riches. *There isn't one.* It *will* provide a common-sense approach to working your investment dollars and managing the risks present in *every* investment vehicle the financial markets have ever created or *will* create. Some investments will work well. Many will not.

You will learn to *maximize your profit* on those that work and *minimize your losses* on those that don't.

You will learn which financial products to avoid as you create an investment strategy that will work for *you,* one based on reality, not on the golden promises and "risk-free" dreams of those many "professionals" out there.

And you will *un*learn all the supposed "rules" financial professionals have been spouting at you since time immemorial. As you go through this learning and unlearning process, you will begin to understand the subterranean game being played *at your expense.*

And you'll adapt and change, armoring yourself with a financial education and developing the skills to assure that your dollars will be working for *you,* not someone else.

How is this book different from the reams of other "investment" books on the shelves?

1. It's written in the same language you learned in high school;

2. It dismantles each investment vehicle into understandable elements and fundamental components;

3. It explains the good news, the bad news, and the bottom line for *you,* the beginning investor;

4. It *really* discusses the bad news—no dancing around the investment downside—as well as the performance upside.

Its readable style will encourage you to keep it on your coffee table rather than next to the "reference books" on that shelf you haven't looked at for years.

It will teach you how to assemble a simple, flexible and diversified investment portfolio with "all-weather protection," the same way you'd build your final home—to last.

It teaches, preaches, and reinforces good money management principles *that haven't changed much in the last 50 years*. Rather than embracing arcane, cockamamie theories economists and investment advisors learn in modern portfolio management classes, it explains what works and what won't work in the *real* world.

It will, like its predecessor, **Get Rich Slow** (Career Press, ISBN 0-934829-71-3, 224 pp., 1990, $8.95) make the financial industry angry because this information is dangerous to *their* financial wealth.

With the exception of ranting and railing against the people out there trying to get *your* money, I have no particular axe to grind. No particular product—mutual funds, CDs, insurance policies or anything else—that I hope to sell you. No seminars to get more of your money. No videotapes on late-night TV. And although I'm a financial planner and am available as such to anyone, I certainly am not encouraging you to "use me" to set up your budget, put together your financial plan, or execute it.

I have written this book to help you learn how much you can do *yourself*. And how important it is for *you* to take control of your own financial destiny.

I am absolutely furious that so many people are taking great delight and making absolute piles of money **ripping you off.** If reading this book saves you money (if it *makes* you money, even better!), that will be more than enough satisfaction for me. And, I hope, for you!

Chapter 1

Your Battle for Investment Survival

GRITS, GRATS, GRUTS, RIPS, SPLITS, STRIPS, LYONS, TIGRS, PIGS, CATS, ILITS, REITS, RELPS, SLOBS, PYGMYS, MIDGETS, GNOMES and LPs.

Encyclopedia entries under "dressmaking" and "zoology?"

A waitress's abbreviations for the daily specials?

A second grader's first spelling test?

No. Believe it or not, this is a typical list of current investment possibilities. With simple-to-understand terms like this, no *wonder* we're confused, even mesmerized, by the myriad of investment products on the market today.

And this is only the beginning. I could go on for days with MECs, SPDAs, SPWL, UL, VUL, IRAs, 401ks, 403bs, TSAs, TDAs, ee-i-ee-i-oh!

Add some devious sales techniques and the greater product knowledge of those in the financial industry (whom we could label, in the spirit of their vehicles, BUFONS, TICOONS, CRKS, SCHNKS, WMPS, SHRMPS and SCAMS), and it's perfectly understandable why many of you would prefer to just roll over and go back to sleep rather than dedicate yourself to learning about investing.

If *you* have been so confounded that you've longed for someone else—*anyone* else—to just *tell you what to do* to solve your retirement, college, and basic investment decisions, this book is for you.

Never bring a knife to a gunfight

Why bother to learn at all?

Because you still remember that last sales presentation when you felt like a mushroom kept in the dark and fed so much propaganda.

Because you feel like a recent graduate of an IQ-reduction course every time you attempt to put yourself in charge of your basic investment decisions.

Because Ed McMahon has not notified you that you are a $10,000,000 winner. And Super Lotto *still* hasn't called.

Because, like most of us, you were born into a nice but relatively poor middle class family with no Uncle Harry to leave you his millions when he died.

Because you have a humongous financial challenge waiting if you intend to fund even a *public* college for your children.

Because the responsibility for accumulating a supplementary pile of retirement dollars nearly as large as today's national debt is resting squarely on your shoulders.

Because you will watch over your money more carefully than any institution or paid individual.

Because you can do a better job of conservative investing than anyone else.

Finally, because financial opportunities may not be limited, but your investment capital and time certainly are.

If you have read my previous book, ***Get Rich Slow,*** you understand that *no one* knows all the answers. But the average investor isn't even equipped to ask the right *questions*. This book will teach you the right questions to ask...and a good many of the right answers, too.

And learn you must. It is far better to paddle your own raft over the rapids than to give up the oars to a stranger, sit down in the bottom of the boat, close your eyes, cross your fingers, and hope for a happy landing.

Likewise, there are better ways to make money than by loaning out *your* money to those who make a *generous* profit if they choose good financial strategies but who *still* profit (from carved-out fees, management expenses, etc.) no matter how horribly they *mis*manage your investment dollars.

That's not what *I* call a partnership, considering *they can't make a dime without* **your** *seed capital.* You take the risk. They get the reward. And you have nothing to say about how the whole thing works.

Interesting concept. Any wonder why there's more month left at the end of the money?

With friends like these

Whoever said "the boss may not always be *right,* but he is *always* the boss" could have expanded on this dogma. The salesperson may not always be telling the truth, the whole truth, and nothing but the truth, but he or she is *always* the salesperson (under such *nom de plumes* as financial planners, investment advisors, retirement specialists, or "senior citizen and elder care specialists"). As such, his or her primary job is to wrestle your signature to the bottom line of a product order form, not necessarily provide you with objective and competent investment advice. No matter what happens to your investment capital, the salesperson always receives his or her commission up front. You alone will either enjoy future benefits or suffer investment losses over the long haul.

This book will dispel and expose biased and subjective sales approaches you have been witness or victim to. So keep it handy, because as you become more highly educated, creative financial marketers will undoubtedly produce more cunning sales approaches to separate you from your money.

Sales pitches that work

Like the basic food groups, there are specific and identifiable groups of sales approaches commonly employed to elicit action on the part of a client and a commission check for a salesperson.

The expert from afar

It has been said that a prophet is never recognized in his own time. Likewise, a financial guru may not be recognized in his or her own immediate neighborhood. By the illusion of distance, however, an otherwise overlooked soothsayer may become more credible. The popularity of investment newsletters from various favorable climates of the country has created positive net worths for numerous financial advisors and investment counselors who might otherwise not have had the opportunity to send so much advice to so many grateful small investors waiting faithfully by their mailboxes.

Advertising brochures vary widely in sophistication and scope, but they generally sound like one of the following:

A. "For a nominal $450 for education materials, you can have my 'right-on-the-money' strategy so you will always be in the right investment at the right time. We had all our subscribers out of the stock market before the 1987 crash."

B. "For only $200 per year my 'Smart Investor' letter for investment cowards will personally let you know how to make it big in only safe investments. Our readers were miles away from the Crash of '87."

C. "For the tiny price of $175 (or 12 itsy-bitsy payments of just $15) you can buy your own personal market timer. We blew the whistle and predicted the '87 Crash."

D. "Learn which stocks, bonds, and mutual funds to shed immediately, and which to gobble up. For $100 per year (an amount so small you won't even miss it out of your monthly Social Security check) you will get my infallible formula and a free copy of my last book, Cleaning Up After Wall Street, a whole year's back issues of my previous predictions, which we overprinted, and a four-pack of tickets to the next seminar I give in your town (not that we need you to fill up the room). Our readers paid no attention when we advised them to get into the stock market several years ago. So they were also out during the Crash."

The critical element of such a promotion is to publish a fancy glossy brochure that conveys the specific concepts they are trying to communicate. By filling sentences with words like "safe," "high yields," "simple," "convenient," "grow rich," "cautious," "ultra-safe," "recession-proof," "urgent" and "low risk," they can appeal to a broad base of uninitiated investors, who feel only a fool or a speculator would go it alone when for just a few dollars they could make millions safely, without ever leaving their recliners.

The similarity between this kind of literature and a carnival barker's *spiel* about the incredible shrinking man, pygmy girl, six-legged calf, and gorilla woman—yours for just 50¢—is striking, but these ads must work or perfectly rational marketers would not use them.

The credibility builder

Wading through the above excrement may be easy for you and best read on an empty stomach, but this next approach is harder to spot and more difficult to counter. If you listen carefully to the sales presentation, you will probably hear one or more of the following phrases designed to reel you in:

1. "If I had lied to my clients, I wouldn't have any."
2. "Here is a list of satisfied clients."
3. "So-and-so bought this from us, and they love it."
4. "I don't do this for the money. I just love working with people."
5. "I won't make a penny on this sale. I'm just thinking of you."
6. "This is exactly what your deceased spouse would have wanted you to do with the insurance money."
7. (Crying—really) "You must buy this! I wouldn't forgive myself if I left here and something happened to you and you weren't covered."
8. "We have five jillion dollars under management."
9. "Our company is so old we make Methuselah look like an adolescent."

10. "That's right, we do it all. We have the best of every-thing."
11. "I'm really a financial planner."
12. "I'm only here to help you. You've got to trust me on this one."

The strategist

Then there are the "mechanics" who cut their teeth selling timeshares in the Himalayan Mountains—mountain hide-aways near the top of Everest. They are good. They are *very* good. They work primarily on emotional appeals and finding your "hot button." The following represents just a portion of their repertoire:

1. "Safe as money in the bank." (Appropriate question to ask: "Which country?")
2. "Your money is liquid 24-hours-a-day. Here is the number in Peru to call."
3. "15%! Guaranteed! Honest!"
4. "First, tell me what you want so that I can tell you we have it."
5. "You want income? You'll have income coming out of your ears."
6. "This is really hot now. Everybody is clamoring for it."
7. "This nursing home policy covers it all."
8. "You are as healthy as a horse. I can tell that just by looking at you."
9. "You better buy it now before it goes even higher."
10. "Don't worry, I can get you insured for anything."
11. "This is how the rich make their money."
12. "I would sell this to my mother." (Probably true.)

Selling the greed motive

These are easy to spot unless you are willing to be deceived into chasing high yields and exorbitant returns without understanding that these come only at a greater expense of your investment capital or at increased risk to your principal:

1. "We'll pay you 10% on your money (what's left after we carve out our share)."
2. "Need short-term money storage at higher yield? This is it."
3. "Look how rich you'll be—not that column, you skeptic, the column I marked in big red letters and dollar signs."
4. "Of course, it's not cheap. You get what you pay for."
5. "This is perfect for you."
6. "This is a vast improvement over what I sold you last year."

The objection overcomer

You may be resistant to the above and want to take your time to research investment alternatives and do some clear-headed thinking, but the good salesperson knows that if he or she can't sell on the closing call, there is a good chance that the sale will never be made. There are only so many arguments in the way of purchasing any product or service, and the objection overcomer has a rebuttal for them all:

1. "Take my word for it, your accountant will love this."
2. "I thought you were the decision-maker in your family, Mr. Prospect."
3. "Why compare? You'll only waste time and buy this anyway."
4. "Read the prospectus first? You won't understand it. Just listen to me."
5. "Pay no attention to this complicated contract. I'll tell you everything important in it."
6. "Don't pay any attention to the fine print. It's just a bunch of words. Something to keep attorneys busy."
7. Don't bother to shop around. No one else would touch you."

8. "Your attorney doesn't understand complex investments."

The tax expert

Some people will do almost anything to avoid paying federal and state income taxes. These magic words—"tax-deductible," "tax-deferred," and "tax-free"—have created millions of sales to people who didn't care whether their investments were in gun running, goldfish breeding, or basket-weaving...*just as long as Uncle Sam didn't get the money, darn it.*

Tax advantages should only be your last consideration, but they are often marketed to disguise otherwise inferior investment products. Beware the salesperson who touts these above all other benefits:

1. "This will sure fool the tax man."
2. "The tax man cometh, and leaveth empty-handed."
3. "This tax shelter is so shrewd that even the government doesn't know about it."
4. "If the IRS questions you on this, tell them to call me."
5. "Who cares what it is? This will save you a fortune in tax dollars."

The closer

Since sales are mainly created by aggressive and assertive efforts, a good salesperson understands that pressure and intimidation may work even if nothing else has. Never allow the following tactics to influence you to purchase a financial product or service until you are completely satisfied and ready to part with your dollars. Defend yourself against the "hard sell," even if it means dropping civilized behavior and doing some intimidating yourself.

1. "I really must know today."
2. "The price is going up tomorrow."

3. "I can't come back."
4. "Why don't we just wrap this up tonight?"
5. "If I knock down the price right now, will you take it?"
6. "If you give this up, you'll be making a terrible mistake."
7. "Even if you sign tonight, you can always cancel it later. It's just an offer to purchase."

All of the above are direct quotes either I or my clients have heard over the years. As blatant as some of them seem, each of them (and more that couldn't be printed even in a PG-rated book) have been used to get a signature on the bottom line. I am sure there are even more creative (or more abhorrent) examples that I have not seen or heard.

A final warning to all readers who hear any of the following: Excuse yourself, see your salesperson to the door, and bar the door for future visits. These are perhaps the most dangerous sales practices of all:

1. "Nope, I can't think of a single think wrong with this investment."
2. "Just sign here. I'll finish this application at the office."
3. "Don't tell the company I am doing you this favor."
4. "You'll never regret this."
5. "This is SAFE."
6. "This is GUARANTEED."
7. "Don't bother reading the contract. You'll be bored to death."
8. "Trust me."
9. "This is so complicated, you'll never understand it."
10. "We are the experts."
11. "We're so big, we have to be good."
12. "You know us (from all the advertising)."
13. "You can trust us (from all the advertising)."
14. "We're like a supermarket. We do it all."

15. "You have more important things to do with your life than to watch your money on a daily basis."
16. "Our reputation is spotless. (Maybe so far)."
17. "You can't get out now. You'll lose too much money."

The main thrusts of selling financial products depends upon greed or fear. Sadly, too many in the financial services industry spend more time in seminars learning to close a sale than learning to utilize their investment products properly and appropriately. Sales pitches work because they appeal to basic instincts. Naivete, gullibility, greed, laziness, and fear can leave you caught in a psychological trap or lead you down a path of illogical thinking.

The object of too many sales presentations is selling the emotional benefits, fostering as few questions or objections as possible, and closing the sale quickly. A good salesperson is not going to allow negative information to influence you out of a sale which he or she has tried so diligently to close. You have the sole responsibility for defending yourself. There is a vested interest on the sales side. There must be an equal survival defense team on your side of the table.

Chapter 2

Meet the Public's Financial Advisors

Numerous surveys have been conducted to determine where consumers solicit investment and money management advice. The response percentages differ from survey to survey, but the same professions invariably make the list—*even though, for the most part, their specialties are totally unrelated to investing and money management.* Here are the groups most people traditionally go to for investment and money advice:

Doctor, Doctor, tell me the news

All too many people believe that physicians are great investment pickers (and that they are becoming even richer by overcharging patients, whose money they immediately wire to their brokers to make even more money). The truth is that many doctors take little time to actively manage their own financial lives. Medical practitioners lost billions of dollars in the limited partnership schemes of the early 1980s, while even more were badly burned on "hot" investments that turned "cold" after physicians traded away their investment dollars.

Medical school never has and, hopefully, never will, offer courses on financial planning or investment strategies and techniques. I, for one, heartily endorse the tradition that the entire curriculum of 12 to 16 years of pre-med, medical school, residency, and specializing continue to concentrate 100% on my body parts—and how to repair them—rather than on a significant number of courses dealing with modern portfolio management.

Your Honor, I resemble that remark

Let me state emphatically and conclusively that some of the most admired professionals I interact with in my practice are lawyers. Additionally, I know how cheaply you attorneys can sue when offended. Thirdly, I had nothing to do with any lawyer jokes ever perpetrated and don't even pass those jokes on to others when they are *really* funny. Like the one when the lawyers were out playing golf and...

Attorneys are, by nature (and seven expensive years of college tuition) profoundly profound individuals who spend a lot of time prefacing every response with, "Although I am not qualified to speak directly on this issue, in the case of..." I know this because I raised one.

It's easy to understand why consumers would believe attorneys can think and talk their way in, out, and around anything, even bad investments. If you were a salesperson, would *you* sell F. Lee Bailey something that could possibly head South?

Some attorneys, after wrestling an opposing side into a large settlement or extracting a favorable verdict, may feel they also owe some responsibility to a client for directing any recently awarded tangible assets. Some clients foster their dependency by showing concern (fear, terror, paralysis) at the thought of taking so much money home in a paper sack and being responsible for its prudent management.

In the world of business, there is a term called "reciprocity," better known to us common folks as "you scratch my back, and I'll scratch yours." So if an attorney recommends a certain individual to assist you in making your investment decisions, gratefully decline any such offer and actively conduct your own interviews and research to find pertinent financial advisors.

"Bankers' hours" just got longer

In case you mistakenly believe you will escape selling pressures and uninvited advances by temporarily depositing your money into a lending institution—while also seeking independent advice from your banker or the securities department—you have just missed the wildest ride Savings & Loans have taken since the Depression.

Bank deposit insurance (FSLIC and FDIC), plus fear of investment losses, used to keep money in banks. With today's insulting CD and savings account rates, that same fear has become anger, with many banking customers voting with their feet.

Lenders are as desperate for your deposits as any other financial product vendor. The only reason they don't greet you on your front porch at 6 am is their image. How would it look for your neighborhood lender to stand in line waiting to see you, tongue out, panting in anticipation and anxiety? Do you think your neighbors would feel comfortable leaving *their* hard-earned cash in such a "secure" bank?

No, your lender has to be content to wait around the branch office and nervously pace through the corridors in hopes of spotting you on your way to the teller window. He or she may spontaneously engage in idle conversation about the weather, your soon-to-mature CDs, your health, his special on interest rates, how clever your poodle looks in ribbons, the bank's latest solvency rating, when the two of you should do lunch (and sign some papers).

For every dollar that walks out of a lending institution, the lender loses the ability to loan out a lot more dollars. Conversely, every dollar that can be snared in a time deposit (such as a CD) is worth far more to your banker than a single dollar. Your banker will be more than happy to give you advice. Just don't expect that your money will be destined for any place other than his or her bank.

Multiply line 8 by the integral of line 42a

The ability to read and understand year-end corporate financial statements, sort out all the important plus and minus figures, and spew out meaningful conclusions has always amazed and impressed me.

I have worked with a number of accountants over the years. Some are brilliant. Then there are some who call me annually to ask why I suggested that their clients purchase a non-deductible IRA. (These live by a simple oath: If you can't deduct it, forget it.) We expect accountants to be knowledgeable enough to deal expertly with *any* type of number problem, even those that deal in concepts, rather than basic cold accounting procedures.

All accountants are *not* tax planners. Most accountants are very careful to avoid being labeled as investment advisors, and their strict adherence to legal and ethical standards of practice prohibit them from reaching beyond their scope of specialized training and background. So do *not* request that your tax advisor prescribe financial planning techniques for your retirement years or decide whether you should invest in zero coupon bonds or growth mutual funds for your child's education.

A perfectly admirable tax maneuver may turn into a future disaster if tax planning is not viewed by the light of more important issues—the purpose or length of time for your investing policy and your choice of the finest investments available.

Planning primarily for tax reduction may destroy the implementation of your primary goals and the real focus of your investment planning.

I see too many crossed bridges that clients were coerced into burning that cannot be built again. Do not paint yourself into tax corners from which you cannot extricate yourself later if the winds of Washington change and blow ill in your tax-planning direction.

There are, of course, some accountants, who believe the cutting-edge portfolio revolves around the nine-month CD. These individuals do not recognize the devastation caused by inflation and focus only on number-crunching and visible dollar losses.

Consider your accountant as a vital part of your financial team and as a reserve against IRS onslaughts, not your "ear on the investment world."

Keep the roof *over* your head

When is the very best time to purchase real estate? Just ask any agent or broker. **Right Now!** This very *minute*. Don't even *think* of having breakfast first! In fact, why are we wasting time standing here discussing details when you could be out viewing homes *because you haven't a moment to lose.*

If interest rates are low (or appear that way), you must buy quickly to lock them in. If rates are reaching for the sky, you should jump in now before they escalate further. Having enough money to purchase a house isn't the problem it once was—that's what creative financing, government money, first-time home buyer subsidies, agent partial commission rebates, assumable mortgages, and parents are for.

The real estate industry makes money *only* when you purchase property and buildings. But you don't have to trust their word and rely on their recommendation alone. Bankers will also agree and be thrilled to offer you large piles of additional mortgage money. Insurance agents think it is splendid that you will need more life insurance and homeowner coverage to go along with your increased debt load.

The government appreciates your assistance in moving the economy along, and will even throw in some games called tax write-offs. And the credit card industry will be more than willing to present you with as many credit cards as you can carry to purchase the home furnishings, kitchen appliances, patio furniture, drapes, and a suitable pedigree pooch. Even the furniture salesperson will want you to purchase a large, *bare,* and roomy chunk of personal real estate.

Can you think of any reason the above would advise you *against* buying your dream house now? Neither can I. So don't expect the traditional realtor or real estate agent to distract you with other investment options such as CDs, insurance products, or mutual funds.

I'm only calling my best customers with this one

Today's stockbroker (more properly called a *registered representative)* has a greater variety of investment options for

your financial challenges. In fact, you name it and he probably has (or can get) it. An accurate slogan for most brokerages might be: "If you want it, we'll hunt it down, create it,
develop it, strip it, dissect it, introduce it, disguise it, or imagine it."

Looking for income? Here is income out your ears!

Need safety? The words "U.S. Government" are printed 51
times in this prospectus.

Want growth? I heard that this could be the next Xerox.

Hate taxes as much as we think you should? Your IRS
worries are over.

Searching for higher yields? This is as high as the numbers go.

You say you want safety, growth, *and* high-yield income...tax-free? I'll just bet we can find it.

There are some registered reps who do a reputable job of
picking portfolio stocks, bonds, and mutual funds for their
clients. I have seen some quality portfolios. Likewise, I have
witnessed some disasters that make the invasion of North
Africa look mild by comparison.

The brokerage business has been so deeply carved up by a
combination of the junk bond debacle, the market crash and
subsequent corrections plus a decrease in merger activity that
only 2/3 of their numbers are left.

The quality of advice varies widely from one firm to another and from one rep to another. Backroom research may be
biased due to the focus or image a firm wants to display or
market. Wealthy clients usually get sweet deals and hot
issues before the average small investor. There is also the
potential of dead issues previously underwritten (bought by
the brokerage earlier on the assumption that they could be
readily sold later) that are gathering dust on the firm's
shelves. If a firm is stuck with unattractive inventory, they
incur losses. If it is sold to a *good* customer, that client will
leave. But if a *small* investor—like you—purchases a mediocre offering, will the firm's future business, reputation, or
image be tarnished or in jeopardy? Not if you only put $2,000 a
year into an IRA.

In general, trading should be reserved for those who can afford to lose money. I always tell clients who want individual issues that I will recommend companies for them if they realize (and sign that they understand) they can lose *all* their money, they know what a monetary loss really is, and they have lost money previously in an adult manner without tears and violence. Otherwise, I recommend mutual funds. There is an argument for some single issues (individual stocks or bonds) but, in my opinion, not in the beginning portfolio of the small investor with limited financial resources.

Since reps are paid only through commissions for their advice (which must produce purchases), a conflict of interest certainly exists. How often do you believe a rep will tell you about a better product elsewhere that he or she is not able to offer? Salespersons have the same problems of feeding their families, finding college tuition, and funding retirement that *you* do. The only place they can earn their money is from our pocketbooks. Given a conflict between a client's interest versus a full grocery cupboard at home, there may be little real competition.

Now, dear, just do what we did

It's easy to assess the quality of financial advice you will receive from your parents without even broaching the subject of money. If they seem financially well-endowed—they're able to travel often, have a comfortable retirement lifestyle, and maintain a well-diversified portfolio of CDs, money market funds, mutual funds, quality stocks or bonds, and even a piece or two of investment property—*listen to whatever they say.* They understand how money works.

If, however, there are constant squabbles about paying bills, worries that they will live long enough to outlive their assets, and concerns about health-care costs, take their advice with the proverbial grain of salt. If they receive most of their monthly income from fixed income vehicles such as Social Security, pension annuities, bank interest and monthly insurance checks, their boat has sailed without them, and they didn't even know how to board. The power of time has vanished, and their dreams and goals have turned to fear.

If you follow the path of these traditions, you cannot expect any more comfortable retirement. Seniors primarily utilized their money over the years for three so-called investments: (1) They bought a home; (2) they put their savings in banks at lower-than-inflation rates; and (3) they gave the remainder of their savings to insurance companies, who paid them even *lower* rates of return and had the use of their money for decades. How well have these institutions served today's retirees?

I rest my case.

You *can* get rich. Just die.

If you have read my first book, **Get Rich Slow,** you already know how skeptical I am about your ability to obtain independent and objective advice from the insurance industry, especially when they are confronted with a large pot of your money glistening across the table. Though I have respect for some fine insurance professionals (in the real sense of the term), so many of them are primarily interested in their own pocketbooks that it is impossible for a novice to tell which one(s) to trust.

A whole life or cash value (savings element) insurance policy makes the greatest commission of any insurance product sold. An insurance annuity pays the next highest commission, while term insurance and mutual funds generally pay the lowest commission rates to an insurance agent or registered representative.

Given these parameters, can you determine how frequently an agent would offer advice at the expense of his or her own family paycheck? Would you even expect an agent to recommend depositing money into a CD or an alternative investment they cannot sell?

There is relatively little regulation in most states. State insurance departments cannot effectively monitor so many licensed agents. So deception can be easily used to induce a sale. If the client and the agent later disagree on what was originally promised, an agent's plausible excuse is that the client misunderstood the agent because this insurance business is so complicated to understand and average consumers don't really understand complex products.

The consumer, however, *always* understands what he or she heard that created the "sizzle," plainly saw the overly attractive ledger sheets that were interpreted as fact (with certain columns of figures highlighted by the agent), and can flawlessly remember the agent's verbal promises that never appeared in the written contract.

Uncle Sam will always be there

Don't depend on the government grasping the reins for long-range financial directives. With a recession facing every official during the 1992 campaign, the last thing a politician worth re-electing would advise you to do right now is to stop your consuming, to stop spending, and to increase your savings habits. Furrowed political foreheads have SPEND, SPEND, SPEND written all over them.

If you save every penny you can get your hands on and stash your money away like a squirrel for your future, that's powerful financial medicine for you. But if *everyone* should get the hang of this kind of budgeting, where would consumer spending dollars come from to keep the economy in autos, homes, appliances, clothes, vacations, entertainment, and other consumer durables?

Someone has to keep this hamster wheel of currency revolving through the economy. So it might as well be you, the average consumer. Call it default planning or short-term political expediency, sporadic sanity and spontaneous spurts of thinking are all we can look toward. After all, look at their own "house budget"—some track record! If your budget were in the red as consistently as the national balance sheet, you would have been forced to declare bankruptcy long ago!

Billions of our tax money shore up sagging thrifts across the nation. The budget has to be balanced (or at least look that way). The trade deficit has to be dealt with or our industry can't sell abroad. Congress is faced with helping Third World countries limp toward capitalism. We just trimmed the defense budget. Should we grab it back again? And by the way, whatever happened to the peace dividend we were supposed to enjoy?

No, this is definitely not the yellow brick road, either to or from Kansas.

Don't look to the wisdom of others to make your money work effectively for your future goals. Take charge, get a financial education, and use the instructions and principles in this book to steer you in the right direction.

Will the Real Financial Planners Please Stand Up?

OK, you're ahead of me. You aren't asking your banker or doctor or attorney for advice. By gum, you want someone out there with some real credentials. You want a real financial planner. You'll show everybody now.

Not so fast. You may be setting yourself up for a long fall.

Anyone reading this book could go into the garage, paint a sign that reads "Financial Planner," and hang up their shingle in their front yard to attract clients. That's how much regulation there is on the use of that term. "Financial planner" sounds more impressive than "salesperson" or "agent," so salespeople often use the term without actually earning that mark or credential.

Real credentials are more than a glossy business card. Real credentials imply two vital foundations: (1) They represent skill levels of competent work in various areas of financial planning; and (2) they denote regulation. An expert may have more letters *after* their name than you have *in* yours. But it is the important credentials you need to ferret out.

This chapter will examine some real and not-so-real labels used in conjunction with the financial industry to create the *illusion* of credibility, competency, and objectivity.

Who's minding the store (house)?

Registered Investment Advisor is a term with little meaning. It only means that the person (or their firm) has registered in Washington, D.C., with the Securities and Exchange Commission (SEC). In other words, you pay your money, you sign up, and you can use the label.

This title does *not* connote the completion of *any* coursework or the successful completion of *any* exams in the financial planning field.

Is this term worth anything at all? If you find that you have been damaged by someone using this title, you can complain to the SEC, who will look into your accusations. But it is very difficult to prove deception or fraud, especially when the hand of greed (yours) signed the application 23 times, acknowledging it had read the prospectus with the word "Risk" printed in bold type in 147 places.

There are several trade industry organizations who police their own members and require certain standards of practice. Most cannot levy penalties such as prison, but they can isolate the "bad apples" by censuring certain members from doing business with the rest of the industry.

One such group is the National Association of Securities Dealers (NASD). They can also handle your customer complaints regarding one of their members and have the power to investigate alleged consumer violations of fraud or deceptive practices. They regulate brokerages as well as their employees and salesforces.

Brokerages are ordered by both the SEC and the NASD to adhere to compliance standards as agreed to by the industry. You can also complain to the SEC directly on any matter of economic loss or some alleged deception under the general securities category. But don't bother complaining to them because you can understand only the title page of your investment prospectus.

Those are regulated by the SEC and followed through by the NASD, and it would take more time than an Act of Congress to convince any member of either group who has spent years learning the secret codes to change them into simple language that anyone could read and understand. Save your breath and just keep struggling through those prospectuses. Someone, somewhere, must know what they mean.

On top of these layers of regulation, there may be state security departments. They are usually very busy because they are all located in urban districts where there are few good parking spots. So employees spend much of their working hours running to the parking meters with change. Use them only for backup; they are very tired.

Since states enact their own securities laws for sales occurring within their boundaries, some have more rigorous rules than others. Some states require competency or state registration testing for financial advisors. Some just want to know if the advisors are still breathing and can sign registration slips. And some just leave you and your advisor alone, believing you don't want to be disturbed at a crucial point in the sales presentation.

Brokerage firms do not make money when their salespeople do not sell product. So don't expect either the firm or the salesforce to hang neon signs above the disadvantages or risks of any product you may seem interested in or be induced into wanting.

Insurance specialists are insurance agents who want you to know they specialize: Whatever you need, they can specialize in it. They range from estate planners (who sell insurance), to investment advisors (who sell insurance to businesses and to families), to "senior care specialists" (who sell all kinds of insurance to the elderly, whether they can hear or not), and pension benefit specialists (who sell insurance packages to companies for use as employee benefits). If found in the wrong sales circumstances, these specialists can often recover fast enough to come up with the right business card at the right time.

Can you find the players without a scorecard?

A *Certified Financial Planner (CFP)* has taken courses and completed exams in six major areas of risk management, comprehensive planning, tax planning, asset allocation, retirement planning, and estate planning. After progressing through these courses, the candidate must pass a two-day comprehensive examination before he or she can use the credentials and the title, Certified Financial Planner.

This curriculum takes approximately two years and is taught and administered by the College of Financial Planning in Denver, Colo. The public can check on a financial planner's credentials, for the College has an active list of those still in good standing and of those whose standing has gone into the toilet.

The International Board of Standards and Practices for Certified Financial Planners (IBCFP), in Denver, regulates all the Certified Financial Planners, who now have to pay annual dues. The IBCFP expects its members to adhere to a code of ethics and disclosure practices. It regulates its members and can exclude any wrongdoers from its membership and publicize their name with a nasty article in every paper they subscribe to.

Admission to the *Registry of Financial Planning Practitioners* (Registry) is awarded by the International Association for Financial Planning in Atlanta, Ga., and is achieved through several steps, including the submission of a comprehensive financial plan and update, interviews with the candidate's clients, and the successful passing of an examination compiled from the current state of financial planning in all areas. The Registry stands separate from the general membership of the International Association for Financial Planning. The public can call for Registry planners in their local areas.

The *Certified Employee Benefits Specialist (CEBS)* designation is offered jointly by the International Foundation of Employee Benefit Plans and the Wharton School, University of Pennsylvania. It normally takes five years to complete and covers the comprehensive format of employee benefits, often leading to a separate career as a benefit specialist in the public or private sectors. Ten courses and their examinations must be successfully completed.

The *Accredited Personal Financial Specialist (APFS)* mandates that candidates hold a Certified Public Accounting degree and have spent 250 hours annually in personal financial planning for the past three years preceding the compulsory six-hour exam. The supporting organization is the American Institute of Certified Public Accountants (AICPA), New York City.

The *National Association of Personal Financial Advisors (NAPFA)* has recently adopted tougher membership standards. The parent organization, located in Grove, Illinois, now requires that a member be primarily engaged in comprehensive financial planning, have a bachelor's degree and additional credits in specific course areas, and offer advice on a fee-only basis.

A *Chartered Life Underwriter (CLU)* is the designation for an insurance agent who has completed six subjects and passed various insurance specialties exams. Don't confuse insurance agents with financial planners. Conferred by The American College in Bryn Mawr, Pa., insurance agents who have earned this designation know everything about how an *insurance product* might creatively fit into your financial life, while planners concentrate on the planning process, which should always come before any product.

Chartered Financial Consultant (ChFC) can be earned by first taking the above CLU courses and then progressing through four more successful exams in related financial planning areas. Although not as well known as the CFP, this mark is considered a financial planning credential. Be careful: With such a heavy insurance background, a ChFC may not look at your financial life from a total planning perspective; there are far more solutions to financial challenges than selling insurance products.

Continuing Education Credits (CEUs) are ongoing annual units of additional education coursework required to keep some certifications and recommended by all industry trade organizations. Maintaining the most current information in such changing areas as investments and tax law brings greater expertise to you, the consumer. You should request a recent list of CEUs from any financial planner you interview.

Certified Fund Specialist (CFS) is the designation awarded by the Institute of Certified Fund Specialists, La Jolla,

California, after completion of study and a national examination regarding mutual funds. This rigorous course separates the generalists from those who have chosen to gain greater expertise in the mutual fund arena.

Today's mutual funds are more integral to the average client's portfolio than ever before. Merely passing an examination to sell them does not provide enough training, given the popularity and number of options to choose from. If possible, find someone who has added this in-depth educational area to their resume.

Registered Financial Planner (RFP) is offered by a trade organization in Ohio whose only membership requirement is the paying of dues. There are *no* educational or credential requirements, so this mark should not be looked on as anything more than membership within an industry group.

The International Association of Financial Planning (IAFP) is another trade organization, in Atlanta, Georgia, whose membership consists of financial planners, accountants, insurance agents, and companies who create and distribute financial products. Membership is open on an annual dues basis.

I urge you to request and examine the credentials of anyone you may consider assisting you in making investments or planning your financial future. We are talking here about an issue as important as brain surgery—your money. If you were diagnosed with a brain tumor that demanded immediate surgery, would you search for a doctor with specialized credentials and a resume a mile long or for someone without an M.D. who volunteered to operate on you because they had a lot of experience around the operating room?

Looking beyond the resume

The more credentials one may possess, the more facts and knowledge in a given area one has at one's disposal to assist you with your financial goals and objectives. But I have known some highly educated individuals, in many pursuits, who could not think their way out of a paper bag. So memorizing facts and regurgitating them at exam times will not guarantee the ability to organize and analyze your problems or to skillfully assemble the various sectors of your financial life into a tight-fitting plan custom designed for you. Even with impressive credentials, there is no guarantee of clinical competence.

Perhaps even more important than credentials are the motives and skills of the financial planner trusted with your dreams and goals. Financial planning is a process, not selling products. It is a dynamic changing relationship between clients and their professional, not a sales presentation with ledger illustrations and brightly colored product brochures.

Real (and good) financial planners do not promote investment products at the first meeting and do not hype you with marketing gimmicks like "tax-free," "tax-deferred," and "tax-deductible." They don't present you with programs that disguise the basic investment vehicles.

A real financial planner cares personally about your welfare, not just where the rubber hits the road (or the pen hits the check). If any money advisor seems more intent on showing you product solutions to your problems than assembling the various pieces of your financial life, find one who cares more about you than about fees or commissions.

The goal should be problem solving, not product selling. Signing applications and picking up commission checks should be subordinated to the process itself. As a client, you should be able to identify many improvements and real progress due to the ongoing communication with your planner. If all you can remember is the investment hype, you are in the wrong office. You should have been taught concepts of wealth building, not fed sugarplums of double-digit returns.

Put them to the test

One way to assess a financial planner is to interview several. Does the planner put you in charge? Do they reveal the inherent disadvantages in all financial products? Does the advisor disclose all fees and charges (even the hidden ones)?

Does he or she encourage you to read and discuss all documents or prospectuses? Did they volunteer specimen contracts to look over at your leisure?

Do you feel pressured to sign on the bottom line? Are you gaining helpful information instead of hearing just a sales pitch? Does any of the information sound too good to be true? Do any promises sound hard to believe?

Is the advice appropriate for your total financial picture? Does the planner always recommend proprietary products (ones that only their company sells)? Do you feel comfortable with this person?

The essence of financial planning is evaluating your strengths and weaknesses, isolating goals and objectives, and providing appropriate options. There are several major areas which a planner should investigate and analyze, whether you are paying a fee or not:

1. *Risk management*—auto, liability, health, disability, homeowner, and death insurance considerations;

2. *Current status*—your cash flow (expenditures) and your Statement of Financial Position (assets, liabilities, and net worth);

3. *Short-term and long-term goals*—including college and/or retirement;

4. *Current tax status*—and general tax planning;

5. *Asset allocation*—your portfolio mix and appropriate investment options, including estimates of Social Security and pension retirement benefits;

6. *Estate planning*—wills, Powers of Attorney, trusts, current ownership and beneficiaries of assets.

A good financial planner won't let you:

1. Borrow more credit card debt than you can really afford.

2. Avoid putting money into an emergency fund, even though it is only a few dollars each month.

3. Buy a house with more than a 15-year or 20-year mortgage.
4. Buy a car for longer than 36 months.
5. Forget that either you work your money or someone else gladly will.
6. Buy into the philosophy of "living today and forgetting tomorrow."
7. Forget that the government is not worried about your retirement; that responsibility is primarily up to you.
8. Believe that a non-deductible IRA isn't worth the extra trouble.
9. Throw some money at your goals, cross your fingers, and hope for a happy financial future.
10. Depend on winning the lottery to solve your future financial challenges.
11. Forget that "time is money." (The time value of money concept is top priority for others who want to work your money for their benefit.)
12. Ignore the reality that inflation is the deadliest long-term money-killer.
13. Convince yourself that you can spend more than you make.
14. Wait another year to take action and put yourself in charge of your own financial destiny.
15. Deceive yourself into believing things will automatically get better with time.
16. Believe in the words "safe" and "guaranteed."
17. Believe in a perfect investment.
18. Take action on financial matters until you have examined all options.
19. Do business with anyone before reading and understanding the written contracts and the fine print.
20. Accomplish the above alone. He or she is willing to assist your research but wants you to remain in charge of your basic financial decisions.

21. Forget that on the road to financial success, where
     you are now is not nearly as important as in which
     direction you are moving.

Good financial planners change fear into education and
peace of mind. Each of my clients is unique. But they are all
honest people raising children with values, hoping to have
something left over for retirement. To me this is a sacred
trust, and it angers me when I see it abused.

I applaud those professionals who sacrifice self-interest in
the interest of their *clients,* and I warn those whose primary
objective is the almighty dollar that, as consumers become
more educated, they will not be tolerated and will be driven
from the marketplace.

What's this about *paying* planners?

Most folks are wary of taking out their own appendixes or
representing themselves in a murder case in court. Financial
planning is every bit as important as brain surgery, every bit
as serious as a lifetime jail sentence.

You can receive all the free advice in the world with one
call to any financial supermarket, insurance company, or
lending institution, all of whom have vested interests in
where you will put your money. Where can you find objective
and competent advice for free?

You need to know the whole truth about your money, not
what is either popular or profitable to someone else. You must
find someone who will direct you where you should be heading, not sell you what you initially think you may want. In
order to receive objective and unbiased money management
information, you may want to pay for it on the same basis that
you pay for the services of any other professional.

Free lunches may cost much more than the menu originally suggested.

Chapter 4

Your Financial Road Map

The purpose of developing a financial plan is to provide a map for you to follow and comfort stops along the way where you can monitor your progress. As you determine your financial goals and objectives, keep in mind some questions to stay on track.

What are your short-term priorities? What are your long-term financial goals? Are they realistic? Can you make the long-term goals by achieving the short-term ones? Are both types of goals working in tandem with each other? How much time have you allotted for each goal? Do you have breathing room in case unexpected life challenges interfere with your optimum plans?

What is your debt picture? Will your goals allow you to live within your economic means? Will they strengthen your future? Do you need the cooperation of others?

Before you can assess where you're going and how you're going to get there—or work with a financial planner to help you find those answers—you need to know, in detail, exactly where you are. Completing and analyzing the following are essential: (1) Your short-term objective plans; (2) your long-term objectives; (3) your current income and outgo; and (4) your total net worth. The worksheets on the following pages will help you compile and organize this information.

Short-Term Financial Goals Worksheet

	Essential	Important	Not Important
Eliminating credit card debt	_____	_____	_____
Taxes	_____	_____	_____
Vacation	_____	_____	_____
Home Furnishings	_____	_____	_____
Medical expenses	_____	_____	_____
College expenses	_____	_____	_____
Emergency fund	_____	_____	_____
Hobbies/collections	_____	_____	_____
_____	_____	_____	_____
_____	_____	_____	_____
_____	_____	_____	_____
_____	_____	_____	_____
_____	_____	_____	_____

Short-term goals are those within a time frame of two to three years. Short-term money must be handled in a special manner because liquidity, flexibility, and accessibility are top priorities. The trade-off will be a decrease in yield. By concentrating on conserving the principal or the safety of the investment capital, you must give up more attractive rates of return.

Long-Term Financial Goals Worksheet

	Essential	Important	Not Important
Retirement funding	_____	_____	_____
New car	_____	_____	_____
New home or condo	_____	_____	_____
Vacation home	_____	_____	_____
Starting a family	_____	_____	_____
Boat/RV	_____	_____	_____
Major home improvements	_____	_____	_____
College education	_____	_____	_____
Child's wedding	_____	_____	_____
Extended vacation	_____	_____	_____
Professional studies	_____	_____	_____
Career change	_____	_____	_____
Starting a business	_____	_____	_____
_____	_____	_____	_____
_____	_____	_____	_____
_____	_____	_____	_____

The goal of long-term dollars must be conservation of *purchasing power,* not principal. If your goals are more than three years away, inflation will loom as your deadliest adversary, and you must plan your investments to beat or at least keep pace with inflationary pressures each and every year. Some growth investments are essential.

Cash Flow Income Worksheet

INCOME

Wages, Salary & Commissions $ _____

Dividends, Interest & Capital Gains $ _____

Rents $ _____

Other $ _____

Total $ _____

OUTGO

Taxes $ _____

Housing $ _____

Food $ _____

Clothing $ _____

Transportation $ _____

Utilities $ _____

Insurance $ _____

Education $ _____

Child care $ _____

Entertainment $ _____

Vacations $ _____

Professional fees $ _____

Gifts, donations, charity $ _____

Miscellaneous $ _____

Savings $ _____

Total $ _____

What Are You Worth?

Liquid Assets

Checking accounts	$_____
Savings accounts	$_____
Money market funds	$_____
Life insurance cash values	$_____
Total Liquid Assets (a)	$_____

Investment Assets

Stocks	$_____
Bonds	$_____
Mutual Funds	$_____
Certificates of Deposit	$_____
Other	$_____

Retirement Plans

IRAs	$_____
401k, 403b, TDA, TSA	$_____
Basic Company Pension	$_____
Other Retirement Plans	$_____
Total Investment Assets (b)	$_____

Personal Assets

Residence	$_____
Vacation home or land	$_____
Cars	$_____

Jewelry/art/antiques $_____

Collections $_____

Other $_____

Total Personal Assets (c) $_____

Total Assets (a + b + c) $_____

Liabilities

Credit card balances $_____

Mortgage $_____

Car loans $_____

Time/personal loan installments $_____

Education loans $_____

Home equity loans $_____

Other $_____

Total Liabilities $_____

Your Net Worth

Total Assets $_____

Minus Total Liabilities $_____

Your Personal Net Worth $_____

Chapter 5

Some Myths of Investing

MYTH #1: Trust me. I'm the expert.

The financial industry's mission is to help itself. To do that, they have to convince you that their product benefits outweigh alternative investments.

Institutions spend billions of advertising dollars annually to access your credibility and your seal of approval when, in fact, their sales forces are trained, pressured, brainwashed, and highly motivated by lucrative missions, to sell, *sell, sell!*

Would any sane car dealer send you across the street after a better overall value? Would any banker voluntarily offer you information regarding better interest rates at another bank? Would a gas station owner suggest you buy gasoline cheaper at the station next door?

Of course not. Agents, representatives, and other salespeople make money only when you buy...from them. That is *their* job—to get your signature on their product agreement. *Your* job, on the other hand, is to ferret your way through all the gimmicks, hype, salespitches, promises, and misinformation to protect your pocketbook and your paycheck dollars.

Beware of well-meaning incompetents

An accountant colleague of mine, Hugh Christensen of California, tells about a young European family during the war who were sent to safety by the husband. He dutifully put his wife and their baby on a train to a neutral country and promised he would join them after the war. As the train lumbered through the night, the young wife became sleepy and asked the conductor for assistance. She needed to get off at the next stop, a town over the neutral border. Would the conductor please wake here in time? He promised he would and, content, she fell asleep quickly, the baby in her arms.

A few hours later, the train slowed and then stopped. But no conductor came to wake up the young mother. A passenger sitting across the aisle, having overheard the original conversation, became concerned. Finally, he shook the young woman and told her the train had stopped. She hurriedly picked up her things, barely stepping off the train before it chugged off. The passenger was pleased with himself but angry with the conductor for being so undependable.

The following morning, the conductor entered the train car, noticing the empty seat where the woman and her baby had sat. The helpful passenger confronted the conductor and chastised him for neglecting such an important request. The conductor flushed. "Our stop last night was merely for picking up water for the engine," he said. "We were deep in the Alps, and there are no towns or shelters in that area. You sent her out into the freezing mountains alone."

At the next town, a search party was sent out. But when they found the mother and the child, it was too late. The elements had taken their toll.

Well-intentioned incompetents can create as much havoc as any self-interested vendor.

Why are they telling *you?*

If someone is a "stock market expert," why are they selling investment advice instead of buying stocks? If they are successful in their careers, why is that so? Is it because they do so well for their clients that they have so many customers? Or is it that they are so good at *selling* that they can bring in lots of business from consumers? The best salesman is not who you want. You are looking for the best financial advisor. You're the reigning expert when it comes to your self-interest and maintaining control over your financial investments.

MYTH #2: Who cares what it is— it will save you taxes

Tax-deferred, tax deductible, and tax-exempt are wildly successful marketing strategies sold today to direct billions of dollars into the coffers of insurance companies, state projects and municipalities. People will do almost *anything* to avoid paying taxes, even lose money.

They will make poor financial decisions in the light of more important criteria. They will encumber their assets and limit future flexibility to re-position/ their dollars over time. They will limit access to their money and incur severe penalties. They will ignore the necessity of outpacing the devastating effects of inflation.

They will unknowingly do *all* the above...just to avoid the taxman.

Instead of being so monomaniacal about taxes, always consider the following priorities (in this order) when investing:

1. The purpose of the investment (an emergency fund, purchasing a home, funding college, saving for retirement, planning a business);

2. The ideal and optimum investment vehicle (money market mutual fund, CD, growth mutual fund, insurance annuity, zero coupon bond, etc.);

3. Tax advantages which will make the optimum investment products look even better (IRA, 401k, 403b, SEP, UGMA, or KEOGH).

A sales pitch to solve your tax problem might also lighten your pocketbook or even alert the IRS. In the early 1980s, doctors, attorneys, and other professionals were induced to purchase tax-favored limited partnerships. They didn't care whether they were investing in real estate in Antarctica, pygmy bonds, or horsefeathers. All they heard was the guarantee to solve their tax burdens. When TAMRA (tax law) changed in 1986, the IRS began to investigate abusive write-off deals and participation agreements with little good economic purposes. Not only did these investors suffer the loss of their tax advantages, but many also eventually owed huge penalties.

Since there is no such thing as a perfect investment (no one ever mentioned that to you during the passion of a sales presentation), you must invariably make compromises to fit your individual financial circumstances. Rarely will all three investment priorities fall in line with your goals. When you make important financial decisions, give up a tax advantage before compromising the other aspects of your investment shopping list.

Short-term dollars must be flexible, liquid, and easily accessible. In order to satisfy those criteria, you will need to sacrifice return or yield for safety of principal and liquidity. Long-term financial objectives must be identified and treated in a totally different manner. For those, you must achieve growth over time because inflation—not loss of principal—is your primary adversary.

Most of the time you will get something for your money. But is it the best investment you can find? A good sales agent is certainly not going to open up any can of worms by telling you more than they need to for your signature. What if you started comparing their products with alternative investments? Maybe you would start asking embarrassing questions about fees, real annual rates of return, commissions, surrender charges, and who's going to manage your money. They don't want to waste a lot of time talking to you all day because there is a long line of more cooperative employees waiting to sign up with outstretched fistfuls of money.

Usually the tax pitch alone is sufficient. You are smug because you beat the taxman, and the sales agent is happy because he or she will make money every time you send a check to their company.

It *does* make a difference whether you are investing in gun-running, bootlegging, goldfish breeding, saving the whales, junk bonds, rare coins, speculative real estate, insurance products, or limited partnerships. In the next few years, pensions will see pressures and fallout like never before. You had better know where your money is invested. And if you are not comfortable, move it. Even if you have to give up some tax icing. The Pension Benefit Guarantee Corporation can not guarantee very many pension plan failures. You have to help protect your money.

Learn to separate the tax shelter from the underlying investment vehicle. Stocks, bonds, savings accounts, CDs, insurance annuities, GICs, and mutual funds are investment products. The *ways* to the means—401ks, 403bs, TSAs, TDAs, IRAs, SEPs and UGMAs—are merely the tax shelter wrapping around the investment to keep Uncle Sam from dipping into your earnings until later.

You never buy a 401k or an IRA. You may, however, purchase a mutual fund or CD in a 401k or IRA wrapper. You can't be sold deferred compensation. You may, instead, be talked into a life insurance policy that postpones taxation until you withdraw the money. ***The investment vehicle is more important that the tax shelter.*** If you must give up something, give back the tax gimmick before sacrificing the quality of the underlying investment.

MYTH #3: You have more important things to do than watch your money—others will be happy to do it for you

Many people depend only on some vague kind of faith instead of solid planning for their financial futures. They naively believe that the new home down payment will appear in time, their child will somehow receive enough financial aid for college, and the government and their companies will come through with a comfortable retirement.

The success of your financial future goals does *not* depend on luck or winning the lottery. It *will* depend on your setting out resolutely to take control of your basic monetary decisions. Good intentions are worthless. Everyone has a reason why they didn't achieve greatness. Nobody will care why you didn't get to the top of your mountain.

Why put someone else in charge of your money? Would *you* have loaned billions of dollars to Latin American emerging countries and then, when they defaulted on loan payments, lent them even *more* money? Don't put the fox in charge of your henhouse or the inmates in charge of the asylum that will house your money machine. You will do a better job and watch over your money more carefully. You will also do a better job of managing it.

Families set few financial goals or the means to reach them. Monetary dreams do not just happen. They are well planned for. Things do not simply get better over time. On the contrary, they generally tend to become worse.

Are you in better or worse shape financially that you were five years ago? Is your percentage of assets over debts increasing or decreasing? Have you planned how to protect yourself against a 6% loss on your earnings per year through inflation? What are your contingency plans in case your present employer flies South with the geese this winter?

If your financial life is slipping away with no significant progress, you must reverse that decline and do at least some simple planning. Learn to be a marathon runner—this will be the longest and most serious race of your life. Structure your financial life for control and flexibility, for comfort instead of speed, for simplicity of management. Then put yourself in charge. And *start today*.

Work your own money, or someone else gladly will.

MYTH #4: No new taxes

Every national election brings back this popular cry. What sane candidate would commit political suicide by openly warning us beforehand that he or she intended to sock it to us, turn off the government money spigot, raise interest rates, and tighten the public's belt? That's as dangerous as teasing your neighbor's pit bull.

Actually, this campaign promise can be more easily kept than suspected. Why should politicians fight with bureaucrats and the public to institute *new* taxes when they can just raise the *old* ones.

We currently are bleeding from taxes on federal, state, local income, capital gains, retail sales, gasoline, Social Security, unemployment, payrolls, luxuries, excise items, probate, estates, inheritances, real estate, school levies, personal property, business licenses, transportation, interstate trade, IRS penalties, overfunded pensions, automobiles, license places, and toilet paper...and I'm just getting warmed up.

I'll bet if someone analyzed the actual percentage of our paychecks consumed by taxation, we would become manic depressives and refuse to work another day of our lives.

So assume the worst: Taxes are here to stay. They will not go away. They will plague you forever. There is a myth going around that after retirement you will be in a lower tax bracket. At least that's what retirement program vendors tell you. Forget it. In order to pay fewer taxes in retirement years, you will be bringing in fewer dollars, eating fewer meals, living a poorer lifestyle...and in big trouble.

Whether you read their lips, their hips, or the price tags on their battleships, politicians will raise taxes for national programs which will be instituted in the next few years. They will cost big bucks. Congratulations! Many are called but you are chosen.

MYTH #5: Get-rich-quick schemes really work!

Actually, they do. But not for you—for the people that sell them!

There are as many investment schemes and scam artists as there are devious minds who would rather connive than work hard for their dollars. Though we know there is no free lunch and few lottery winners, millions of folks fall for get-rich-schemes and themes that are bogus at best, perhaps even illegitimate, but so enticing that they just can't be ignored.

Most schemes quack very loudly if you listen. If it quacks like a duck, waddles like a duck, but wears turkey feathers, it may be the same old bird dressed up in a new disguise. These schemes offer quick profits, little or no expertise or specific knowledge, and usually sound too good to be true. Pitchmen promise quick returns with little or no risk.

The pitch looks real enough to be believable, and promises are designed to activate your hot button. If something looks easy, it becomes more attractive to the victim. The less mental work or education required, the better the offer may sound.

The leader or investment guru may claim to be a million-aire. The company's offices are usually located in another state. The offer may come via a phone call, a letter, or through a TV "info-mercial" (a long commercial designed to appear educational).

Most offers are only "for a limited time"—to create a sense of urgency that will fuel your greed motive and tempt you to act on emotion. Offers may include public testimonials to add credibility and legitimize the solicitation. They may be folks whose entire lives were changed simply because they re-turned a postcard, listened to a presentation, or invested on the ground floor of an exciting business opportunity.

Some offers suggest approval or sanction by consumer advocacy groups, the Federal Government, or charitable foundations. Artwork is carefully designed with American patriotic symbols that sell the American dream of striking it rich. Carefully selected brochures and phrases are supposed to move you from the couch to your phone or to your check-book.

Too frequently, these offers have little merit. These schemes must work—for their *marketers*—or they would not be so prolific. The recurring question you must ask is: Why would a stranger be letting me in on the ground floor of any-thing? Why would anyone call me, a random citizen in another state, and share the secret to instant and permanent wealth? Why aren't they investing every dime of their own and keeping this magic formula secret?

Dialing for dollars

Boilerplate operations, consisting of rented office rooms filled with paid phone operators, solicit consumers day and night. This is a numbers game. The more calls one makes, the more suckers can be found. An illegitimate company targets an area, sets up its backroom shop, and starts dialing for dollars. In a couple of weeks, it moves and begins a similar scheme in another part of the country.

Never, never, never purchase anything over the phone that is solicited without your prior inquiry. Even if you have previously sent for information, don't buy investment products or items from unknown persons. Any solid business opportunity can be found at a reputable investment company in your area...and they'll still be there next month.

Never give your Social Security number, credit card numbers, or other personal private information over the phone. You have no idea to whom you are talking. If the company is legitimate, they will send you literature if requested so you can check them out through state agencies and other means.

Do not purchase securities, Certificates of Deposit or other types of securities or insurance products from credit card offers, monthly statements, TV, or radio solicitations. These may offer inferior protection or have risks which you won't understand. Nothing is worth jumping into. If an investment is of good quality, it will still be available at a later date. Shun any and all pressures to buy.

If someone tells you that you have won a trip or any other type of prize, request that they send it and pay all shipping and handling costs. Reputable contests don't expect their winners to pay for shipping and other expenses. The money you send may be worth more than the prize when it finally arrives...if it ever does.

Real contests have other means of contacting you and verifying that they are legitimate sweepstakes or competitions. If you have not recently entered a contest, how could you have won?

Ponzi schemes

Mr. Ponzi, a small con man, graduated to rubber-check passing until he struck paydirt by concocting a plan in foreign stamps. Not that any foreign stamp was ever purchased or sold. No, a Ponzi scheme—yes, he achieved immortality—can come in any package but is remarkably simple: Promise large short-term profits to investors. Continue selling new investors, using their money to pay those remarkable returns to the old investors. Keep using the "success stories" of the first investors to get even more new investors...you get the idea.

All schemes topple, as Ponzi's did, and when his roof fell in, he was indicted for mail fraud, conspiracy, grand larceny, and numerous civil suits by conned investors.

There are no large quick profits without great risk. Mr. Ponzi finally died a pauper in a Rio charity ward, but not before he bilked thousands of small investors out of their savings.

Whether you are offered a windfall in diamonds, silver, stamps, or any other tangible or security, apply the common-sense sniff test: Does it smell too good to be true? Perhaps it is.

Chapter 6

The Laws
of Investing

LAW #1: It's a jungle out there

Have you ever thought about the difference between a lion and a gazelle?

Every morning in Africa, a frightened gazelle wakes up. She knows that she must run fast, or she will be killed and eaten.

Every morning an African lion also awakens. He knows that he must run fast—faster than the gazelle—or he will eat nothing and eventually starve to death.

The moral? Whether you see yourself as a lion in the financial jungle or a gazelle timidly picking your way over the rocky terrain, when the sun comes up on another day, you had better be up and running.

Companies spend billions of dollars each and every year just to stalk you (it's called prospecting)—to learn how to target your wants, your secret desires, your hot-buttons, your vulnerabilities, and your weaknesses. You are classified as young, mid-age, pre-retired, or retired; by income level; by zip code; by number of children and their ages; by gender and race; even by sucker lists. You are being statistically followed, tagged, and ticketed like some form of wildlife to be sold to someone's telephone, presentation, or direct mail list.

If you bought a new home, several insurance companies know—they buy the mortgage recording lists from your local area or state. If you take out a personal loan, other vendors are notified. If you recently lost a spouse, every salesperson in town has learned it from the newspaper obituary. If you were recently married, you have been erased off some lists and added to others. A new baby or a college graduate media notice will bring out the car, yacht, insurance and credit card mailings. There are major chains whose cash registers will not open unless you, the customer, provide either your zip code or your telephone number.

When you purchase a lemon of a car, a refrigerator, or a toaster, it doesn't take you long to discover that you have a major problem. You either force the manufacturer to replace it or you sell it off to some unsuspecting victim. In either case, you have diagnosed and solved your problem.

But if you purchase a *financial* lemon, and don't understand it, you may *never* know it won't work until you need it...and that will be too late.

The greatest slogan I ever heard came from a TV advertisement: "We want your business so badly that we are willing to lose a little on each sale and make it up on volume." (Think about it!)

Why in the world would you believe for one micro-second that any of these salespeople would ever show you any glitch or negative that might talk you *out* of the sale they have sweated and worked so diligently to talk you *into?* They are not working with church bingo money here. This is serious business. This is next week's groceries, next semester's college tuition, or the family vacation in Bermuda that they have promised their spouse and kids.

There are few *slow* veteran safari hunters.

LAW #2: Where you are on the road to financial success is not as important as which direction you are moving

Even if you start now, it is possible to fall short of your financial goals. But if you never start, you are doomed from the beginning. Time is money (or the loss of it).

If you waste your money, someone can help you. But if you waste your time, no one can buy back that precious commodity for you. There will never be a better time, a cheaper time, or a more important time to start—than today.

LAW #3: The best defense is a good offense

It doesn't take a rocket scientist to control and manage your financial life and destiny. It does, however, take some common sense, thought, a skeptical investigative mind, and more than fifteen minutes per year to develop a working plan you can understand and stick with.

The inventor of financial planning was the ant who worked through the summer gathering up stores of food so he would be secure when winter arrived. The grasshopper, however, thought this type of goal-setting a complete waste of perfectly good recreational time. He spent his summer and fall eating, lounging on wild aster plants, and having tobacco spitting contests with his neighbors. He didn't notice the shortening days and the meadow plants losing their leaves and color as the fall nights became colder and colder.

When the first snow hit without warning, the grasshopper immediately jumped into action and scurried to the ant's home. He pleaded for shelter, but there was no response. Then he demanded refuge from the storm's onslaught and some of the bread he could smell baking in the ant oven. Again he was ignored.

In desperation, he battered in the anthill's front entranceway, deciding to take his destiny into his own hands. But he was so fat from dining on milkweed and grain pods all season that he could not slip down through the corridor. There he stuck, somewhere between salvation and certain death.

This was a prime example of poor planning—consuming everything today and saving nothing for tomorrow. It was exactly this kind of tragedy that financial planning was designed to avoid.

The only things that go away when ignored are your teeth. Financial challenges and problems must be addressed, tackled and solved.

LAW #4: Learn to think like the rich

The middle class has developed a demeaned concept of $1.00. To them, a dollar represents a cup of coffee, a pair of shoelaces, or a lottery ticket. They also see little reason to ferociously protect it.

The affluent, however, view a dollar as the means of making more money. They have well trained mercenary instincts (or well-paid consultants or both). They know that if they can keep turning that dollar over and over, it will continue to grow for them and create $2, $4, $8, and even $16, given enough time.

To be successful, you have to begin to think like the rich and value every dollar for what it can eventually become—more dollars—*if* you hang on to it and work it yourself.

LAW #5: Every potential sale is inherently an adversarial situation

Not every financial salesperson is a crook, and not all of the honest ones are incompetent. But how can you, a novice, tell the difference? Don't let personal relationships or friendly conversations interfere with your thinking processes regarding which options may be in your best interests. Salespeople want to anticipate what you are looking for, so they show you products they think you want. Many of them also lobby for specific products which have large commission checks attached.

You must separate the emotional appeal—the sizzle—from the real overall value—the steak—and, after taking your time to research and compare, determine your own financial direction, the bottom line. If you calculate the cost of a financial education as too expensive, consider well the alternative price of your continued ignorance.

LAW #6: With accurate information, money will follow

Financial planning is not only for the rich. The truth is that the less money you have to manage, the more important it is to use it wisely and get objective and competent advice.

Like the bus driver who constantly complains that he can't meet his scheduled timetable because he has to keep stopping to pick up passengers, the facts are evident, the logic is impeccable, but the argument is totally false. There must be a better solution.

Reprogramming your mind to think like the institutions will dictate using good money management fundamentals, not just learned responses, a common substitute for using brain cells.

LAW #7: It's what you make on your money after inflation that really matters

If I told you that, as one of my best clients, I would offer you a special investment that was worth $1,000 in 1945, had steadily and consistently declined in value each and every year since then, and was now selling at $140, would you be so anxious to purchase it from me? That is what inflation has done to the American dollar.

Inflation is the deadliest money-killer over long periods of time, as dangerous as any other loss of principal. Because inflation erodes money away quietly, it is largely ignored by consumers, but certainly not by institutions and corporations who use your savings or who lend you money. They clearly understand that they must consistently outpace inflation.

Inflation will never go away. No one taught your parents about its ravages, and too many of them learned the hard way—they became its victims. People worry about lung cancer from contact smoke, cholesterol in their eggs, nuclear radiation from power plants and x-rays, while this insidious erosion quietly eats away at your financial futures, destroying your comfortable retirement and your children's college educations.

Never forget that the return on investment is less important than your return after inflation.

LAW #8: Preserving your long-term purchasing power is more important than preserving your investment principal

Ignoring inflation is financial suicide. If inflation averages 6% per year, you must yield 6% (after taxes) on your money *just to stay in the same place* you were at the beginning of the year. If inflation is *greater* than 6%, you must receive an even higher return...just to continue treading water. You must always receive more on your money than inflation eats away in order to make real progress.

The longer your money works below inflation, the more seed money you will use up. Each year you will gain less interest because there is less money to receive interest *on*.

The effect of inflation on wages is even more unsettling. If it takes $30,000 per year today to keep your family and home together, in ten years, at 6% inflation, you will need $53,725 per year to retain the same purchasing power and lifestyle you now enjoy. In twenty years, you will need $96,214 per year. Where are you going to find that kind of money? Can you count on big-enough raises to earn that kind of salary? Those increases to continue your current living standards will not come by loaning out your money on a charitable basis to others.

Whether you are young or retired on a fixed income, you must beat inflation with your long-term savings. Of all the guarantees you may hear about, the one no one selling fixed interest investments talks about is the guaranteed *loss* over time which you will sustain. Fixed income vehicles have *not* generally kept pace with inflation over long periods.

LAW #9: S-A-F-E is a four-letter word...and a big lie

Risk is everywhere. You cannot escape it. So you'd better learn to manage it.

The risk most feared by investors is loss of principal. In fact, folks tend to concentrate so heavily on securing their investment principal that they actually guarantee the very risks they so intensely seek to avoid. You will eventually go broke if you leave all your money in "safe" investments like CDs, government bonds or fixed insurance annuities.

"Safe" banks and "safe" insurance companies purchase long-term bonds, the kind that go way down when interest rates go way up. They also buy junk bonds, some of which don't go way down but actually disappear before your very eyes. They also have liked real estate, the investment we recently learned doesn't always make money. And they can choose some equities (stocks), which everyone knows go up and down all the time.

You have pieces of paper with lifetime (bank and insurance company) guarantees. Those guarantees are based on the lifetime of the insurance companies or the health of the banking industry. A paper tiger unravels eventually. Guaranteed funds can't save institutions if the very institutions who are supposed to throw large premiums into the pot during a financial crisis don't have the money to do so because they are busy bailing out their own boats.

Please explain to me how anyone can believe a written piece of paper backed by investments that can tank as badly as these have in the last few years? Smoke and mirrors, mirrors and smoke.

By diversifying, you will learn to differentiate between various types of risks and plan for them. There are business, market, interest rate, inflation, and financial risks to consider. Resist the dangerous urge to hide your head in the sand when it comes to promises of "safe" and "guaranteed."

LAW #10: 1. Diversify; 2. Diversify; 3. Diversify

Like the real estate axiom—location, location, location— whether you have a beginning or a substantial investment portfolio, you need to put your money into many baskets. These baskets must also be of different kinds. If you invest in 90 companies, but all 90 produce dining room furniture, you are not really diversified—if that single industry slumps, so do *all* your investments.

Good financial planning and money management techniques haven't changed much in the last fifty years. It has *always* been diversify, diversify, diversify! There will be boom and then the terminal bust, the defiance of gravity and then the sobering reality that enduring laws are prescribed by physicists, not Wall Street hopefuls.

LAW #11: Even a paper loss is a real loss

Your investment fundamentals should be strong, and your specific investment choices should be boring, dull and passive. Don't seek excitement with your important money. A three-year return of +10%, +10% and +10% is better than +20%, +20%, and -20%. If you lose significant investment capital, it will take time to build up your total assets back to where they were.

A piece of comforting advice that brokers give you when you suffer losses is to hold on because you only have a "paper loss" until you sell. This may be consoling, but it is also a lie. They really mean one of the following:

1. No one is perfect;

2. My company wanted me to get rid of that—you just came along;

3. I'm as shocked as you are (only not as poor);

4. I'm glad that was your money and not mine;

5. Did I get my commission up front?

6. You should act like an adult about this;

7. Everyone loses someone else's money sometime;

8. You have some money left—care to try again?

Did you have paper profits before you had losses? Your broker or mutual fund was bragging about how well you were doing with them and hyping the performance records and their positions in the consumer magazines. So you must have had real money *then*. Now you have less money. You have lost some *real money*. That money is gone forever.

The idea of a paper loss is as bogus as calling crashes or mini-crashes "corrections" so as not to upset you with the semantics. A similar parallel can be drawn when the obstetrician tells a woman going into labor that she will experience "some discomfort." No matter what the bedside manner, crashes or corrections are painful things to be avoided.

All losses are real whether you can see them or not. Losses against inflation, taxes and increased risk of principal can be avoided as you learn to manage your portfolio. You need some downside protection against the financial storms but to retain the ability to participate on the profit side. You can't do that if your entire portfolio is locked into equity mutual funds or all fixed-income vehicles.

LAW #12: There is no such thing as a free lunch

There are also few sexy, intelligent, and sensitive men who iron. (But that's another book.)

No one will ever invest your money for nothing, and claims to the contrary should make you nervous. No one will ever offer you a greater return than necessary to induce you to hand over your dollars—not the banking industry, insurance corporations, private institutions, or even your federal government.

Don't shop for high yields. They are come-ons. Once upon a time we thought getting a 14% bond was good investing savvy. Then we learned the meaning of the word "junk." Higher *yields* can only be bought at higher *risk* to principal.

There is no safe 20%, 15%, or even 10% return. Anyone who tells you there is will profit from your greed and naivete. There are no secret formulas to riches that you will be offered at rock bottom prices. If these dog-and-pony shows were accurate, all the professionals would buy the secrets and sell them to their clients at a mark-up.

There is no status in overpaying. Cheaper often means inferior. But paying more doesn't guarantee better quality. There is a tremendous difference in costs for comparable investments. As you shop, you will find large discrepancies.

The more overhead you pay, the lower your net rate of return. The greater the commission, the less you get. The more profit a company wants, the smaller the pie piece left for you. Scrutinize alternative vehicles before making long-term decisions. Purchase the best, not the most expensive.

LAW #13: Investment performance is determined by P-R-O-F-I-T-S, not P-R-O-P-H-E-T-S

Shakespeare once wrote that no soothsayer (fortune teller) should ever be able to look at another soothsayer without breaking into laughter. How can one predict reactions and future events created by events which haven't happened yet? People are often right for the wrong reasons. Only the successful recommendation is publicized. The dynamics and logic leading to the prediction are rarely investigated.

Who can predict a war, a famine, or even a recession accurately? Experts in this country fiddled around with the "R" word for six months before anyone had enough data (and gumption) to actually reinforce what workers and consumers had already known for the previous six months—we were in a recession.

Prophets predict at the beginning of a year or a business cycle, while profits are realized at the end of the year or the season. Hindsight is much more accurate, though a prophet makes more money by predicting the event.

Small investors are nearly always wrong. They get in at the peak of someone else's profits because they have spent time watching others make money and now they feel safe. Then they turn and run away at the first sign of trouble or decline. Small investors work primarily on greed and fear.

Unfortunately, it's hard to think on your feet with your adrenalin pumping and your heart pounding in your ears.

Develop a long-term investment attitude by choosing quality for your investment challenges and diversifying the heck out of your money. Once your portfolio is constructed, *leave it alone*. Investors run after the hottest yield or the latest double digit superstar mutual fund and destroy the very planning that will hold together during distressed periods. They jump to something else they have been watching gain profits. Soon after selling what they owned and buying the new vehicle, it plateaus, and what they *left* suddenly jumpstarts. They spend so much time watching other opportunities that they ignore the strength and wisdom of managing their current portfolios.

Flamboyance is not necessary and not advisable. More fruitful and productive are taking your time to pick out your portfolio, selecting your options, carefully putting each piece into place, and being responsible for making your basic investment moves. Monitor your investments on a semi-annual basis (if you assembled your portfolio properly, you don't need to micro-manage on a daily or monthly basis) just to be sure things are working as you desire.

The get-rich-quick, nothing-down, wealth-without-risk themes and schemes attract millions because they appeal to greed, laziness, ignorance, and naivete.

It is hard work to make those original seed paycheck dollars, and it's going to take some hard thinking to keep those dollars working primarily for you. Anyone who stands out in a field looking for a sign from above will attract lightning and crows (and vultures who prey on the naive and defenseless).

If you are looking for a winning formula or for secrets to financial success, your best answers are not around you. They are within you. The world is not full of wisdom. It is populated with sheep, followers, cunning marketers, and fools. Follow your own common sense, and seek answers through logical and clear thought processes.

LAW #14: It's not what they say, it's what you sign

When you receive an insurance or securities contract, take the time to read it carefully. You should always request a specimen contract *before* your purchase. If not, at least read your contract carefully through after you receive it. Never take only an agent's word that you are insured or that your money has been properly delivered.

Always get a receipt, and never make out a check to an individual or to a third-party corporation, no matter how plausible the reason. Never, *never, **never*** give anyone cash. This is untraceable, and such a request should activate clanging bells.

Never buy investment products through the mail or via your credit card statement. You won't know what you are buying, and you cannot depend on the reputation of a company issuing the credit card in many circumstances. They may be solicited just like you are, and they may pick up a distribution fee for every sale that is made through their solicitations. Everyone likes a profit, and they may not know any more about a product or service than you do.

Never purchase anything over the phone. You have no idea whether you are talking to a legitimate company or a boiler-room operation that was set up to clean up and move out before the month is over. Deal through local companies with solid reputations.

LAW #15: There are no fair or friendly contracts

The bold print giveth, but the fine print may taketh away.

Why would any company write so small that you need an amoeba who speaks English to translate it, if they didn't intend to hide the contents from you? Why bother to include it at all?

Because the consumer protection laws insist on vendors telling you certain negative information, but they don't regulate how readable that information must be. When I see print that small, I know it's important.

I am never impressed by the bells and whistles of an investment or written product contract. I head straight toward the risks, limitations, and exclusions. Follow the asterisk. Whenever you see an asterisk, you know there is some "nasty" hidden somewhere in the contract language which may invalidate the claim just made. I have seen sales literature whose fine print waived every single benefit proposed in the preceding clauses. Long-term care policies are notorious for making promises in one paragraph and waiving those same promises in different language in the following one.

Don't buy anything unless you understand what you are buying. And don't get the entire translation from the sales agent. If you later decide that your limited partnership with a 15% guarantee has gone up the chimney, you will be shown your signature and asked if you are over the age of majority. If your signature is not a forgery, the next question ought to be why you are signing things you don't understand.

Pleading total ignorance (or insanity) of what you signed will be no excuse and no defense. You paid your money, and you took your chances. You should have read your contract.

LAW #16: Never invest out of greed or fear

Bulls can make money, and bears can find profits. But pigs wind up with nothing. If you remove the bulls and bears from good basic investing, one thing is for sure—you will have a lot less manure to wade through.

Making money should be boring, *boring,* **boring!** People have locked into the idea that successful financiers and money moguls are the celebrities we see publicized in the tabloids, making their daily rounds to pick up a large check at one stop, sacks of dollars at another, and reproducing their megamillions because they take huge risks.

These show-offs perpetuate their reputations by pretending everything they touch turns to gold. They are only on a temporary roll, but we can imagine ourselves attending black-tie functions and rubbing elbows with the super-rich, just like they do.

Structure your portfolio for comfort, not for speed. If you need some excitement, get it through your bowling night or golf game. Let your assets slowly compound over time, staying afloat during distressed business cycles. The financial world will market anything they believe they can induce you to buy.

Unless you are a trader or want to be actively engaged in managing your investment portfolio, find good professional management underneath vehicles such as mutual funds, and monitor your money markets and bank CDs yourself. Outguessing the market will just add up to volatility and could obliterate your basic investment strategies.

The only way to turn a sow's ear into a silk purse is to begin with a silk sow. Always purchase quality. Never invest by fad or hype. You may feel you can pick the next IBM, but more likely you will invest in Fred's Guitars, which fades soon after you buy it...at its all-time high.

Large investors, the kind that don't wince at buying $100,000 of something at a time, spend more time than *we* have researching, have greater access to timely information, and can implement more clever investment strategies than we know. And sometimes even *they* lose big. It is the nature of this arena. This is serious business to the pros. Don't attempt to match wits with your monthly mutual fund magazine as your investment guide.

You can't beat the market. *So don't try.* Do what you do well—make the investment dollars with your skills (on the job), then manage your investments conservatively.

Chapter 7

Teaching Your Child the Value of Money

I recently wrote and developed a state 4-H project book and course focusing on teenage money management. The greatest difficulty in this project research was discovering sources of teenage earned income. To put it bluntly, *they don't have any.* They pester their parents when they need funding, and otherwise assertive adults dutifully sell another pint of blood to satisfy their children's insatiable monetary appetite.

Your high school or college graduate will be among the slowest group of moving targets ever to be set upon by the financial industry. Credit cards, new cars, homes, furniture, clothes, entertainment, and vacations—standards of consumption and lifestyles they never believed possible at their ages—will be theirs for the stroke of a pen.

Today's adolescents are so ill-equipped to handle the pressures from accommodating salespeople that they may be artfully separated from their first paychecks, from their investment dollars and, in some sad cases, from their future goals and dreams.

I frequently speak to high schools and teenage community groups on the fundamentals of practical money management, demonstrating the permanently destructive effects of inflation by actually burning a dollar bill solicited from my audience. During a recent high school Career Day presentation, I requested a dollar bill from the students for my ever-popular flaming demonstration. Not one teenager in the room had a dollar bill. Oh, they had *ten* and *twenty* dollar bills, but no George Washingtons. (In adult seminars, I am sometimes hard-pressed to solicit even a *five* dollar bill.) Take a good look at your household. You may make the money, but you probably don't spend most of it. At least not if you have kids.

12 Mistakes your children will be tempted to make

1. Living now, paying later
2. Procrastinating
3. Paying themselves last
4. Abusing OPM (Other People's Money)
5. Believing advertising
6. Reading only the bold print
7. Purchasing a "Talking Horse"
8. Failing to plan
9. Mistreating checking accounts
10. Embracing credit cards
11. Never learning the time value of money
12. Ignoring inflation

Nancy Reagan actually had some good advice

It is destructive for parents to provide teenagers with all their spending money, because then the kids learn nothing regarding financial compromises and saving habits. A parent can be more instructive by "just saying no." (Thank you, Nancy.) If your teenagers believe they can refresh themselves from your bottomless well each time they feel a financial desire or suffer a short-term deficit, they will not be prepared when they leave home with a limited income to face crucial decisions affecting their financial health.

Do *not* protect your children from the financial realities of the outside world and from budget constraints within your family. This is their only chance to learn money management skills. Education will teach them techniques to make money, but not how to manage it. They will quickly covet the enjoyment of spending but not the satisfaction of saving. With uncontrolled freedom to be inducted into the world of credit cards, checking accounts, and finance agreements, there comes responsibility—the discipline to understand the promises they've made and the accountability to which they've committed themselves. Observing the financial world around us, they will certainly have few role models to teach them these values. No one is born with the innate ability to manage money. It must be taught.

Out of financial order

Developing a simple budget is a must, even for young adults, in today's economy. The immediate awareness of how money is directed will create better financial consumer habits. A budget doesn't take time; it saves time. A budget doesn't prevent people from having the material things they desire; it allows them to set priorities and, therefore, to achieve those goals. A budget reveals a written record of their expenditures, which can be analyzed and improved. The ultimate goal—satisfaction from every dollar they earn, save, and spend.

It is important to bring your entire family into your money management activities of saving, goal-setting, and investing. It is absolutely vital that your children understand that you are no longer a "tree with money growing out of your ears." Asking your children for suggestions to reduce expenses may often pleasantly surprise you.

The most poignant example of money management comes from you, their role models. Encourage your teenagers to become involved with the family's financial objectives. Hands-on experience is the best teacher—your children will gain real-life practice and feel that their involvement is needed and helpful. Creating a family financial goal can enhance any theoretical knowledge and reinforce the importance of the concepts absorbed.

Teaching your kids the money game

Price is the actual dollar amount agreed upon by a willing buyer and willing seller, each knowing all the facts. The seller nearly always knows the advantages and disadvantages of the item, product, or service he or she is selling. The buyer must determine what is accurate information or he or she will have paid for less value than originally agreed upon.

There is a natural tendency to believe that the higher the asking price of an object, the greater value it must possess. That is often *not* the case. Whether you are buying a melon at the supermarket or a car at an auto dealership, you can pay too much for too little. Comparison and prior research before purchases are the only protection against paying too much in the marketplace.

Most folks would not throw money away. In fact, some consumers, who would fight for a 75¢ coupon on the supermarket floor, unwittingly let hundreds and thousands of dollars flow through their fingers to others because they have not learned to become good negotiators. Not every purchase should be thought of as a purely economic and analytical decision. But if your children typically "fall in love with" the items they buy, they are buying on emotion and will not always receive equal value for the loss of their dollars.

A fancy paint job on an auto may be a diversion to steer them away from examining under the hood. Everyone gets stuck with a "lemon" once in a while. But avoiding costly mistakes is more beneficial than learning expensive lessons.

Smart consumers examine many things:

1. The price of the item
2. The quality of the product
3. How long the purchase will last
4. How durable the product is
5. How often the item will be used
6. How necessary the purchase is
7. The opportunity cost of buying this specific purchase
8. Whether they need this item now
9. If they can afford this item now
10. What other associated costs may be involved (such as maintenance, insurance, or necessary accessories)

When opportunity knocks

Opportunity cost is the key to wise money management and receiving the greatest value for existing dollars. If they have $100 and spend it all on clothes, their *opportunity cost* is all the *other* things they could have done with the $100. In other words, every *lost* opportunity to use their $100 for other benefits.

Opportunity cost does not imply that what they do with their money is either good or bad. It only means that once they have spent their money, they have lost every *other* opportunity to use it again in the future. Since they have only one opportunity to decide how to use many of their dollars, decisions that pass their money to others permanently should be viewed carefully.

Spending and saving mistakes

Does this describe your kids?

1. They see money only as a means to buy something right now
2. Money burns a hole in their pockets until it is spent
3. They purchase many things but seldom derive long-term pleasure from their purchases
4. Saving is not important to them
5. They spend more than they save
6. Spending money makes them happy
7. If they had $1,000, they would feel rich
8. They can only save long enough to purchase small items
9. They believe money is not powerful and has little potential

Read over the above list one more time and put yourself in their shoes. Does this sound as though we are talking to you, their adult mentor? For too many adults in this country, the above list is a carbon copy of *their* attitudes regarding money.

The best savers in this country are three-year-olds. How tragic to realize that from age four on, our children spend proportionately more than they will ever save!

The most creative excuse I ever heard for spending it all today came from a five-year-old who told me he was robbing his piggy bank for some toy he had wanted because "he owed it to himself." Where do you think he heard *that* one?

Saving and spending are not conflicting goals. All saving really means is *not* spending today so one can have more money to spend tomorrow.

Would you take the talking horse?

A long time ago a king was auditioning court jesters. One candidate came forward and announced to the king that he could, within one year, teach the king's horse how to talk. Obviously, everyone in the castle was astonished, and the candidate immediately got the job of court jester.

As the new jester left the throne room, his assistant admitted that he, too, was very impressed that the jester was so talented that he could even teach an animal how to talk.

The new jester turned to his assistant, smiled, and replied: "My friend, a year has 365 days and nights. Each day has 24 hours. A lot could happen during those thousands of hours. The king could die. The horse could die. Even I could be killed. The kingdom could be lost in battle.

"And, who knows, the doggone horse might even learn how to talk. In the meantime, we have a nice life for a year...if we don't rock the boat."

This illustration emphasizes the fact that your children need to learn that promises made during the emotion of a sale must backed up on paper, so *they* don't buy a "talking horse."

We don't back it; we just print it

A strange sense of confidence is what really backs our paper money, and we may have communicated this to our children. If they have little respect for paper dollars, they may have even less esteem for small rectangular perforated tear-out sheets with blue bunnies, yellow chickens or peaceful mountain scenes printed on them. We adults call these "checks."

Someone must teach them that checks are real dollars spent; they carry the same responsibility of spending real money. You can't spend real dollars if you don't have them in your pocket, and they can't write checks when they don't have sufficient dollars in their checking accounts. Opening a checking account is easy. Learning to manage the record-keeping and taking responsibility for the privileges takes some education and money savvy. A checking account should not make them feel richer than they really are. It should not tempt them to spend more than their account balance. It should not increase their spending habits because it is so convenient. It *must* not cause them to spend indiscriminately and without good purpose.

Paying themselves first

Out of every paycheck a portion should go into some form of savings. Teach them the *time value of money*—the greater the time allowed for their money to compound, the fewer dollars they will need to earmark toward each financial goal. (My previous book, *Get Rich Slow*, is a wedding gift-must for any newly married couple or other youth you care about financially.) Like brushing their teeth when they were very young, saving also can become a habit over time.

Your children need to establish an emergency or "rainy day" fund as early as possible. The lack of one is the start of most young adults' problems. Since they have no emergency fund, they begin to borrow cash advances on their credit cards. This becomes a habit and a quick solution to short-term financial problems. The habit becomes a necessity instead of a luxury, and they become hooked on credit. No longer able to afford to pay off the debt with their limited income, they become content with making only monthly payments, believing that the price of a new purchase is not $100, but only $12 per month. Once their thinking becomes flawed, it becomes impossible to climb out of consumer debt until a real crisis forces them to deal with the problem or until they are so deeply in debt that it takes major financial surgery or even bankruptcy proceedings to make them whole once again.

If you teach them nothing else about money, instruct them that if they cannot afford to pay off their short-term debt in thirty days, they certainly cannot afford to buy even more money that must eventually be paid back.

Inflation and interest

Inflation is the most deadly money killer over time. They must learn that conserving future purchasing power is more important than conserving principal. It's not what they make on their money that will count, but what they make above inflation that will really matter.

Show them how to get interested in interest. Compound interest will work either for them or against them. When they loan money by investing, they want the greatest rate of return for their efforts and their opportunity cost. When they borrow money, they want to purchase it at the lowest cost.

Money is a commodity just like a toaster and a lawnmower that is purchased at different prices. They must learn to shop for prices on money like they will shop for a new TV or a new car.

The most vivid method teaching a teenager about compound interest can be accomplished with a scrap of paper and a pencil. Using the *Rule of 72,* illustrate the future value of any lump sum over time. (Divide 72 by the interest rate. The result is the number of years it will take your money to double; e.g., money invested at 8% doubles every 9 years.)

Those friendly credit card people

My definition of a credit card is the industry's permission to allow them to purchase something they don't need right now, at a price they cannot afford right now, with money they don't have right now and, unfortunately, may never make. It is very clever marketing to convince someone to pay more and more each day for something that is worth less and less.

A credit card can be a valuable tool, like a hammer to a carpenter. But if your children start nailing down everything in sight because they expect to immediately move into the same lifestyle you sweated many years to achieve, they will eventually learn some hard lessons.

The most destructive and dangerous personal financial problem facing today's consumers is "credit card crunch." Neither countries nor households can borrow themselves into future prosperity, and consumers are borrowing money they haven't made yet. If a credit card makes them feel richer than they are, it will become the most dangerous enemy they will meet. Credit card abuse can be hazardous to their future financial wealth. Credit isn't a birthright. It's a privilege they must protect.

Questions your child must answer
before receiving a credit card

1. What is the annual fee?
2. What is the annual percentage interest rate?
3. What is the grace period after purchase before interest starts?
4. Is there a charge for late payments?
5. Are there extra fees for each purchase or transaction?
6. What is the annual percentage rate for cash advances?
7. When does interest start after I receive a cash advance?
8. Is there a special fee for cash advances?
9. What does the lender charge for over-the-limit purchases?
10. Are there any other agreements in the fine print?
11. Have I read every word on the application?
12. Have I understood every word I read on the application?
13. Can I afford a credit card now?
14. Do I have enough income to immediately pay for all new purchases?
15. What credit limit do I want to request?
16. What credit limit can I afford?
17. How will this new financial obligation affect existing loans and obligations?
18. Will this convenient method of spending interfere with my saving habits?
19. Will this credit card encourage me to feel richer, to spend more than I would without it?
20. If I begin to spend too much, will I understand I must stop spending and pay off my total balance before using my credit again?

Chapter 8

The Suddenly
Single Investor

If you or someone you care about has been divorced, widowed, or is otherwise newly independent, please read this chapter carefully or pass the information along.

And please don't think this is a chapter "For Women Only." While we traditionally conceive of women in these circumstances, I personally know several husbands who don't dare sign their own paychecks or monthly pension checks for fear of being indicted for fraudulent check signing—their wives have taken care of all financial matters throughout their married lives. So the challenge of facing major financial decisions alone is definitely not gender-based.

This book should give you plenty of encouragement, confidence and money management skills to control your own major decisions, along with sufficient effective strategies to be in charge of any affairs you may have to deal with quickly. At first, planning will consist of adapting and functioning solely from day to day, but realize that these efforts, no matter how paltry and hard, will help you construct a new foundation on which to rebuild your life, both personally and financially.

First and foremost, take your time. There will be days when you have the winning lottery ticket, drive to work on nothing but green lights, and can't find a new gray hair in the bathroom mirror. There will also be those "other" times when you walk into the kitchen to make morning coffee, open the refrigerator, and break a carton of eggs on the floor. While kneeling with a towel to clean up, you slip on the raw yolk and shells, and coat your new-bought business clothes with freshly made meringue.

I'm not Dear Abby, but...

Although this book is designed to help you with your financial strategies, be sure to solicit support in the personal areas of your life. My single clients have compiled these helpful tips—personal advice and nuggets of wisdom that comforted them until they felt both feet were actually touching solid earth again:

1. Blame someone else for everything bad that has happened to you. The instinctive response is to blame yourself, which will quickly destroy your remaining self-confidence. It is far better to blame others for your current plight. U.S. Government bureaucrats have fine-tuned this technique into an art. It can work for you, too.

2. Start watching soap operas. Just by comparison, your life will look brighter.

3. Don't feel you have to "put on a happy face" for others. There is no one more important right now to impress than yourself. If your close friends do not understand, this is a good time to know where they stand...so you can write them out of your will.

4. Don't let your grown children control your life (or move in with you or even convince you to move in with them) to protect you from all the dangers of the outside world. This will stifle your independent growth. They have merely forgotten who protected *them* for thirty or forty years from those dangers.

Tell friends and family members you appreciate their personal attention and support and their listening when you ask them to. But, if necessary, also encourage *them* to "butt out" unless you call them.

Don't set up unrealistic expectations. When holding onto the side of a mountain, *hanging on* is a considerable victory. Allow yourself the mood swings you may experience. Expecting to feel normal or throwing yourself into your job or compulsively into activities may only delay the healing process that is slowly working, though you may not overtly realize it.

Keeping "experts," relatives and friends at bay

Now for the financial advice...and the good news: If you are physically healthy and mentally alert, you are capable of managing and directing your own financial life.

True, you may face decisions for which you are not prepared—insurance company death benefits, company pension plans, alimony, lump sum divorce settlements, retirement fund checks, disability benefits, or even Social Security (fully insured workers' spouses are entitled to a one-time $255 death benefit sum) as well as other types of unexpected money.

This will trigger another coincidental event: Lines of creditors, financial "advisors," insurance agents (even the agent who delivers any death benefits to you), bankers, pension consultants, senior citizen or "elder care" specialists, investment "advisors" and "counselors" will create a traffic jam on your front lawn. These unselfish and anxiously waiting "volunteers" will gladly offer to assist you in making your most important financial decisions—and, of course, automatically disagree with any place you suggest investing your money...unless it is with their company.

If this entourage bears a striking resemblance to circling vultures following a thirsty man across a desert, go with your instincts. Hasty decisions with the money needed to buy your bread and butter and supply you with laundromat change for the remainder of your life will undoubtedly be regretted. They may also be irreversible. Although you may initially feel grateful that an "expert" has come to your aid and lifted this burden from your shoulders, this frenzied pack of "advisors" may be more interested in lifting your wallet or pocketbook.

You will also receive well-intentioned financial advice from relatives, including your own grown children. Ignore everyone right now. Buying on the advice of others (even well-meaning incompetents you may love) is ill-advised. They may have no idea of what they are really investing in (most folks don't).

Unless you have inherited millions (in which case you are probably not reading this book but are on the phone to several financial planners you can purchase around the clock to assure their competence and their loyalty), you can manage your affairs by diversifying into simple investment vehicles you will be able to understand and carefully watch over.

This is not the time to make lasting and perhaps irrevocable financial decisions. Put your money into three-month CDs at several banks, separated into three different piles:

1. One account with all IRA accounts, 403bs, 401ks, or other voluntary supplemental retirement money;

2. A second account containing all basic pension roll-overs that can remain tax-deferred even though they will be transferred to your name. Ask the company benefit staff person to document which money can be rolled over into an IRA account for continued advantageous tax deferment); and

3. A temporary *third* CD account for all taxable money—death and disability benefits, alimony settlements, property settlements, and other dollars—that cannot be tax-deferred and will continue to earn taxable income.

Do *not* co-mingle these separate categories of funds or you will have created adverse tax consequences that you didn't *have* to create. As you deposit the qualified money (pension vesting and IRA money), immediately label those two accounts as IRA rollovers. Eventually, you will make a final transfer of these tax-deferred assets to other investment vehicles.

You may make one IRA rollover on each account per year by actually taking possession of the dollars (called constructive receipt), but you can make as many changes or transfers to various investments as often as you like by simply designating that the money be transferred directly to a new custodian (the fiduciary or trustee behind the new investment product).

These temporary short-term money pots are created to allow you the time to gather information and do some thorough research before you decide on some "final resting places" for your money. If you do not feel comfortable permanently allocating your funds after three months (when the CDs mature), purchase *another* set of three-month CDs, for as much of your account as you still feel hesitant about, to give you more breathing space and more time.

Do not deposit all your CD money into just *one* banking institution (despite the supposed backing of the FDIC). If a bank is taken over by the Resolution Trust Corporation, there may be some disruption of your account marketability (the ability to get your cash out quickly).

Get the right advice...at the right time

Now, you will need the financial cram course of your life. Stay away from public seminars and don't call insurance agents, stockbrokers, financial advisors, or even bank trust or estate planning departments. These all represent vested interests. Pigs will fly before you can be sure you have received objective financial advice.

Do not expect your accountant or attorney to direct you or to provide investment advice. This is not their bailiwick, and there is the possibility that there may be an ongoing business relationship between your legal or accounting professional and a financial institution or company in your community. You are perfectly capable of finding your own materials and interviewing your own money experts. You can subscribe to a few good monthly consumer magazines and give yourself a thorough financial education.

As you feel more comfortable repositioning your assets, keep the allocations simple, flexible, and manageable. This book should give you a good perspective on what will work for *you* on a permanent basis. Read, listen, and ask uncomfortable and probing questions.

As you become familiar with investment vehicles, try one small lump sum at a time, and keep track of your dollars to see how the product works in both bad and good economic climates. Do *not* feel pressured into investing large amounts of your funds until you are fully prepared to commit.

Above all, diversify, diversify, diversify. Don't place all your assets into one or two investments, no matter how good the salespeople paint the benefits. If any investment product is of true long-term quality, it will still be available in a few months or even next year when you add to your account.

Your financial health depends on your decisions. Don't hurry. Don't surrender control for the convenience of lifting this responsibility from your shoulders.

Tell everyone who volunteers to be "helpful" or pressures you for an appointment, that you are sailing to Nova Scotia to save the seals and you won't be back for six months. Tell them you will call them when you return.

Your choice of short-term storage pots is limited because you need relative marketability (the ability to get to your money fast) and total liquidity (assurance that each dollar you deposit will still be there when you withdraw it) in a few months. Therefore, you will be relegated to lower interest vehicles such as bank CDs and money market mutual funds backed only by U.S. Government bills, notes, bonds and other agency paper. These low returns are currently depressing, and you will be tempted to opt for higher yields that promoters of other products offer you. But you are purchasing something right now more comforting than high yields—some time and vital breathing room to learn and research.

Don't be so concerned with the yield on this short-term money that you forget about bank solvency. Be prepared to sacrifice a few dollars in interest for the peace of mind of keeping your money in the strongest, safest bank you can find.

Don't be so *un*concerned with your yield, though, that you deposit your funds into a low-interest passbook account. Find some reasonably competitive 90-day CDs, money market demand accounts, or U.S. Government money market mutual funds for these three separate sets of money. Then start your money education by reading this book thoroughly and doing some independent thinking.

Life goes on...so must you

Find all important-looking papers (including homeowner and auto insurance declarations, utility bills and other monthly commitments) on the kitchen table and sort through them. Buy inexpensive files for each category. Purchase a large desk calendar with large blank spaces and record all incoming monthly money (such as paychecks, Social Security, insurance annuities, or pension checks) in green and all outgoing bills (fixed and variable payments) in red. You can plan as far as one month ahead, but biting off small goals at first in two-week increments may work better, especially if this is a new experience.

This kind of tracking will require less real thinking and will save time. Check your desk calendar each week to see which bills must be paid. Write out those checks and move on to other, more positive parts of your day.

Continue to pay regular living expenses like the mortgage or rent, utilities, credit cards and car payments—no matter how unmotivated you are. Your credit rating is at risk here, and most bill collectors care more about their account ledgers than your problems. Don't use plastic solutions for psychological short-term fulfillment. Loading up credit cards will only present you with another problem months later.

A suddenly single individual may find him- or herself in new territory regarding checking accounts or ongoing automatic investment programs. Halt all continuing programs without penalties, and get to someone (your banker, a friend, or a consumer community agency) who will teach you some basics about handling day-to-day money matters. Don't be afraid to ask for help. Be smart, realizing that it's not important to know every answer, just where to *find* the answers.

Cut down on unnecessary paperwork and consolidate checking or savings accounts. Frequently, spouses have separate financial lives, and you may have inherited another system of money managing. Call several institutions and check on their current rates of savings passbooks, interest-bearing checking accounts, money market demand accounts, or senior citizen benefits. Then pool the dollars into a few areas: one savings account or money market, one checking account, etc.

Do not use long-term CDs at this time because if you need greater liquidity for unplanned expenses, you won't be able to withdraw your money without penalties. There will be some time later to decide on long-term investment strategies. Do *not* make long-term investment decisions now.

Keep most of your funds liquid, because being alone may require more immediate dollars and some monthly income until you have done your long-term financial planning. Don't become sold on purchasing income investments, such as bonds, tax-free mutual funds, insurance annuities, muni bonds, or even limited partnerships. All of these have unacceptable risks as short-term investment vehicles.

Stay away from product salespeople at this time. Concentrate on getting through each day successfully and on getting a good financial education. In the meantime, you can get all the income you need from your checking, money market, or savings accounts.

Do not take on any major financial debts or projects now. No remodeling, no children's financial problems, and no long-term financial decisions. Don't co-sign or otherwise lend any of your new assets to relatives or children. You may need them later, and the promised repayments may not materialize. Your children are probably in better financial shape than you are anyway. They have their youth and healthy bodies with which to w-o-r-k.

Get your own personal credit immediately if you don't already have a credit history. This is vital because there still is discrimination against women or self-employed workers. Get at least one major credit card in your name only and charge occasionally so you can show a history of actually using the card. Be sure to pay off any total balances within the grace period. Even charging a $10 item a few times a year will help. Don't charge anything that can't be paid off during the 25 or 30-day grace period.

As tax time rolls around, get to an accountant to help you through the first year, and to teach you how to do this yourself. Major tax service companies offer current tax preparation courses. These may help. Don't let money, columns of figures, or new financial experiences intimidate you. Take everything one step at a time. You survived this far in life. You can certainly learn a few new skills for better financial living. Community colleges may also offer short courses.

Many folks think that $100,000 or $150,000 in hand at one time makes them rich. Do not be fooled and lulled into taking life easy and gifting away future dollars that you will need. Consider staying employed or being re-trained for a career you would enjoy. This is healthful for you physically and mentally and will get you back into the mainstream and out of isolation faster. Some spouses have been secured behind the walls of homemaking for so many years that they are terrified to start a new lifestyle. Get career counseling, some support counseling, and find positive friends to bounce ideas off.

Get some re-training at your county adult education center, community college, or other outreach extension program format. Apply for any grants that may subsidize your education. Initiating a structured education will put you onto a type of treadmill that will provide a direction and push you along.

Keep your self-confidence up. You may have been working on the indentured servant plan while raising your children and taking care of an entire household, perhaps even while working outside your home. It may seem you were the unwilling, leading the unknowing, doing the impossible, for the ungrateful. Therefore, you should have been doing so much with so little for so long, that you are finally qualified to do anything with nothing.

A large inviting and vacant home (yours) may be very attractive to grown children, other relatives, or co-workers who are wading through a streak of bad luck. Don't get involved. You are not a YWCA or the United Way. You are one person taking your time to get your act together. You can do that best with your own space and with your own breathing room and schedule. You need fewer pressures now...and *no* additional costs.

Change the beneficiaries on all life insurance policies at work and on your own individual contracts. Don't let any agent talk you into changing existing policies and purchasing new ones. Consider carefully your current position before buying any more life insurance or keeping those you own.

Don't let any insurance agent use fear to talk you into a life insurance policy. Think this out. If you have a few bills, own your own home, and have some retirement savings or investments, why do you need death insurance? Your problem now is not dying too soon but living too long. You need your dollars for daily living. Your estate will satisfy your bills after you die.

If, however, you are still responsible for raising children you need a bundle of cheap term insurance. Otherwise, save your money for your own needs, not the commission needs of an insurance salesperson.

Check on spousal benefit options such as ERISA or COBRA health benefits, company pension plans and Social Security benefits. Apply immediately because processing takes time, and, in the meantime, you will be using your dollars instead of those you can qualify for from others. If you shop for your own health or disability policies, compare "apples to apples." Request specimen contracts, and ask several agents to recommend policy types.

To the newly divorced (or divorcing)

There are three elements to each and every divorce: (1) the legal ramifications; (2) the financial consequences; and (3) the emotional arena. Don't expect your attorney to assist you with more than the legal portion. Here you have an expert to walk you through the unknowns and the frightening nuances.

Although the legal aspects tend to overshadow the others, they may be the *simplest* areas to deal with. The psychological and financial aspects, though, may be longlasting—you may need advice from a psychologist and a divorce planning financial planner to help you plan best for your own future.

Too often, the wrong person gets the house in a divorce QDRO (settlement agreement) and must sell it within the year because there is not enough income to maintain such a dwelling. There are hard dollars and soft dollars. If a portion of retirement assets will later be received by you, how can you reduce the risk of time and the possibility that the death of an ex-spouse or their remarriage will leave you without needed funds at your retirement?

What are the tax ramifications of all divorce transfers? Tax rules change, and you need to know not only your legal rights, but also the financial implications of any potentially irreversible decisions you may make. Health benefits may be a problem without spousal coverage. COBRA can bridge such a gap, but you may not be able to fund the entire premium by yourself. What if you are unhealthy?

If you received stocks or bonds as part of a divorce settlement, unique tax consequences apply. Whenever you sell the stock, you will pay the full difference between the original price and whatever the fair market price is on the date you sell it. So you will not benefit from the full market value of many investments. A good accountant can help you in this somewhat confusing area. But don't ask your CPA for investment advice. That should be your decision, and one based on more important criteria than just good tax planning.

Chapter 9

Retirement Myths Can be Hazardous to Your Future Financial Health

Conservation of principal should be a retirement fund's #1 priority

Conservation of *purchasing power* should rank as the primary objective of any retirement plan. Inflation is the deadliest money-killer over long periods of time and is a guaranteed loss of principal, as dangerous as any other potential loss. It's not what you make on your money that counts; it's what you make above inflation that really matters. Regardless of your age, you must achieve some growth on your investment portfolio. Fixed income vehicles alone—CDs, government bills, notes, or bonds, corporate bonds, Munis, zero coupon bonds, and insurance fixed annuities—will not by themselves outpace inflation. Growth without undue risk should be your retirement investment objective.

What happened to my parents won't happen to me

Wishful thinking maybe? Everyone thinks he or she won't be one of the unlucky victims. Statistics don't frighten people into action anymore. Folks don't actively plan to fail in later life. They simply fail to plan. The last generation put their money primarily into three places: a home, banks, and insurance policies and annuities. They were not taught what inflation would do to their savings over time or what they could accomplish if, instead, they worked their own investments.

If you follow this unhealthy tradition, you cannot expect any happier ending. The only retirees currently financially comfortable and independent are those who watched after their own money and worked it for their own benefit.

I won't need as much money when I retire

The only bills that will disappear at retirement are the home mortgage and the excruciating college tuition you may now be experiencing. Inflation won't stop, even though your current income and raises will (replaced by a smaller monthly pension—if you're lucky—with little or no cost-of-living adjustment). Your dentist won't fill cavities anymore—he'll present you with a whole new set of teeth. Income, property, school, gasoline, and other federal, state, local and user taxes will continue upward. The cost of groceries, medical prescriptions, treatments, and other senior services will continue to escalate. You will live longer, perhaps even long enough to outlive your retirement nest egg. Like an older home, you will also need more upkeep.

I will pay few income taxes after retirement so I can live on less

To pay for the large current bills we owe as a society and future costs of health care and increased social benefits, the price of all levels of government will continue to *escalate*. If you intend to be in a lower income tax bracket than you currently are, you will be living on *less* money than you are today. Therefore, you will be in *worse* financial shape. You had better *not* be paying less in taxes, or you will be dieting, whether you want to or not.

I have social security and my company pension to depend on

Years ago our government had an idyllic vision—to tax current workers and pay supplemental benefits to elderly former workers and their spouses, who wouldn't live long anyway. There were so many workers and so few retirees that this concept looked feasible.

Then America began to gray, and workers got older but poorer. As the largest generation yet heads toward retirement, who will be replacing the lucrative industrial jobs to fund larger Social Security payments and contributing enough for this mass of humanity destined to live another twenty-five years after retiring? Not even our government can tax future workers enough to pay for the rest of us who will be retired, disabled, or indigent.

The government tends to respond in favor of political expediency instead of long-term planning. If the government isn't working on your long-term retirement and you aren't seriously saving, apparently you expect your employer to pick up the slack in needed retirement benefits for you.

Business CEOs are at least as intelligent strategists as politicians, and corporations are working hard to stave off governmental mandates and increased pressures from other sources, such as unions.

The inescapable conclusion means that retirement benefits will come from your company pension (if it is still solvent), subsidized by some social security (if it is still there for the middle class), with the remainder of the funds as your responsibility.

It will be easier to save for retirement in a few years

The fallacy in this mode of thinking relies on the hope that you can invest future income that will not be needed as disposable dollars, college tuition, a larger home, raising more children, more expensive cars, and to fund an increased standard of living. If you can't find the relatively small contributions *today* to fund your retirement, how will you ever earmark even *greater* sums in five or ten years (after you have lost some power of the compounding of time), when additional drains on your income may leave you in even *worse* financial shape?

I'm still young—I have plenty of time to save for retirement

Time is money, and compound interest is the eighth wonder of the world. The more time you have to compound your retirement funds, the fewer original investment dollars will need to be saved.

Assume your goal at age 65 is to accumulate a lump sum of $100,000, and you expect to be able to earn 10% annually on all money you invest.

If you start at age 25, you will need to contribute only $16 per month.

Wait until you're 35, and you will need to stash $44 per month.

Waiting until 45 will cost you $131 per month.

If you hold off until you're 55, you will be desperately seeking $484 per month to invest.

By letting compound interest over a long period of time do most of the work, you can achieve your financial goals much more easily...and with much less money.

I'm too old to start now

OK, so you're not 25. But if you do nothing but wait longer, your problem will become even larger, and your goal even more unreachable. Waste your money and someone can help you. Waste your time and no can buy it back. You are running the most serious race of your life, whether as a volunteer ahead of the pack or as a victim pulled along by the deadly effects of inflation and increasing costs for health care, housing, consumer products, and services you will depend on as you mature. The time to start seriously saving is always *now!*

There will only be the two of us

Don't be too sure. Today, more older "boomerang" children are moving back home (often with their *own* children) due to divorce, the death of an underinsured spouse, or as a single parent with a child. Today's grown children are also waiting longer to marry and leave home. Even if you do manage to move your children out, you will hopefully have grandchildren and the desire to ply them with gifts or assist in their educational dreams.

The equity in my home is my retirement fund

Observing recent home sales—sticker shock in reverse—we have soberly admitted real estate prices don't always go up. At best, they will barely keep pace with inflation. But as home prices increase, so does the cost of living. With retirement funding, you must *outpace* inflation, not just keep up with it. You will not fund your retirement based principally on your home's appreciation. Not in the '90s, anyway.

When your liquid retirement assets are consumed, how will you eat? By selling off a bedroom or a bathroom? You will need a comfortable roof over your head and a comfortable feeling in your stomach from eating three meals a day. You need other investments that don't depend directly on inflation for future benefits.

If I save everything today and then die young, I won't have any fun living

If you save 10% of your income for retirement, you'll have 90% left over for wonderful adventures. If you can't live comfortably on 90% of your income today, you are overspending and overconsuming. If you can't stand putting aside some instant gratification today and must spend everything now, how will you feel if you *don't die* and have only the bygone memories of dollars spent, rather than the continued ability to spend something all your life?

Saving and spending are not conflicting goals. Saving is merely not spending right *now*, today, so that we can have more to spend tomorrow.

There is no guarded secret to retirement planning. If you spend all your money now, you will have nothing left for the future. If you become so addicted to spending today, how will you live when you have only photos of vacations, entertainment cocktail napkins and souvenirs, designer clothing long out of fashion, luxury autos that are now rusty, and older status trappings that won't impress anyone?

You *can* have everything, but you may not be able to afford to have everything *now*.

Chapter 10

The Penthouse or the Poorhouse

Let's try some motivation. Close your eyes and picture yourself on the 18th hole of the most beautiful golf course you've ever played. Your spouse waits for you at beachside, while the tropical sun slowly turns both of you a golden brown.

Lay back and dream of California, Florida, Maui, or the Maine coastline, imagining lazy mornings, extended evening dining, and meeting new friends, free from the pressures of work, children, and the current rat race. That's the good news.

Now turn your mind to another scene. You and your spouse are arguing again over the expenses. She is frightened, and you can't seem to make your fixed pension and Social Security checks stretch any further. You rarely talk anymore without lashing out at each other.

Bills lie in a pile on the desk, unpaid from last month. Doctors, dentists, and other specialists want their money. This month's Social Security check has not yet come. There is little happiness in Mudville today. That's the bad news.

Whether your retirement is good news or bad news is up to you. Choosing (and getting) the former will be made easier with the facts and information in this chapter.

How much money will you need?

Realistically, you will need 75% to 80% of your current income. One of the major mistakes in projecting income needs for the next twenty or thirty years is to *under*estimate. So if you think you can live on a lot less, re-read the retirement myths in the preceding chapter. Just how much sooner than the date of your funeral do you want to be broke? I know the answer to that. It is far better to be generous when planning the remainder of your life. If you have "too much," your family will benefit. If you have too *little,* no one will benefit.

The worksheet on page 109 will help you calculate how much you need to save each year to fund the kind of retirement you're dreaming of. It assumes that your investments will grow at 8% per year, and that inflation will continue at 5% on an annual basis. Medical costs will be a major factor. Don't expect Medicare or Social Security to bridge all the gaps. A large segment of the population is groping toward retirement age together. Remember that this is also a gross rate of return, not yet shrunk down by the taxman.

Even if most of your investments are taxable, you should be able to gross, before-tax, a blended return of 10% with a mix of CDs, money market mutual funds, and mutual funds that offer growth potential. All amounts are in today's dollars. So you should update this worksheet annually to keep your savings consistent with your needs.

Money building should be B-O-R-I-N-G

As I've stressed throughout this book, you must come to terms with inalienable realities: You must choose between safety of principal and safety of purchasing power. *You cannot achieve both,* unless you have a lot more money to throw toward retirement funding than most folks can afford.

You must learn to take some risk of principal and use the concepts developed in this book to keep ahead of inflation. You must also move as close to your investment as you can and stop paying these middlemen who do nothing more for you than feed you falsehoods, present salespitches, and try to frighten you with fear of loss.

Some of your money will need to remain in bank CDs in order to establish diversification, and your liquid money can be stored in money market U.S. government agency mutual funds (not the simulated types banks offer). But the remainder of your money had better go into a combination of stocks and bonds to get you increased diversification and growth potential. That means mutual funds, and probably not the ones your retirement plan specialist (salesperson) has been recommending while hanging around the plant, the hospital, the school cafeteria, or the country club pool.

Mutual funds offer one huge advantage over everything else: They allow you to accumulate a miniature diversified portfolio without having the million dollars to spread around in lots of money pots. Not all mutual funds are created equal, and we will learn that the most productive in constantly changing and uncertain economic environments are those which themselves invest in CDs, money markets, blue chip stocks, corporate bonds, and long-term U.S. Government bonds. They come with their own diversification packed into every share.

These are not the glamorous funds. They never show up on the mutual fund hit parade when times are good. They will never outpace the stock funds during bull markets. They never surge ahead like the sector funds, which may have ninety different companies, all of them in building dining furniture. That is not real diversification, it's more like a roller coaster ride ready for boarding.

These diversified mutual funds—called *equity income funds*—are slow to move, dull, passive and stodgy. They only are visible once in a while—during a crisis. When times are bad and investors panicking, these funds quietly surface, floating to the top and riding out the storms. They are the true all-weather pros, performing year after year without nearly enough attention from either the media or greedy investors.

Chapter 17 is devoted to mutual funds—what they are, what they can do, how to separate the best from the list, and how to develop a long-term portfolio in the most cost-effective manner. You may not always be in the top one, but you will be close enough to achieve the goals you have set for retirement. Given enough time and your patience as an intelligent investor, these should form the foundation of your retirement portfolio. Send your insurance agents, your brokers, and the other salespeople who have been living off you a "bon voyage" card, and start building your own ship, to last, with you as captain.

To max or not to max? That is the pension.

When retirement nears, you will begin to wrestle with the pension options available for your employee benefit package. You may have the following choices:

1. A lump sum distribution to continue tax-deferred if rolled over into an IRA labeled account;
2. A monthly pension check for the rest of your life (a one-life annuity);
3. A smaller monthly pension check for the remainder of both you and your spouse's life (joint and survivor annuity).

You may believe this is a difficult decision, but your local insurance agents will already know which option is best for you. They will automatically recommend that you take the larger monthly pension payment and purchase an insurance policy on your life with your spouse as the beneficiary. They will show you how to afford it with the larger check that will come in every month.

There will be the usual impressive ledger sheets that really are meaningless, but which will hopefully convince you that no matter how you feel about it, the insurance company is going out of its way to offer rock-bottom prices and huge annual returns for your relatively small offering—the insurance premium.

Gracefully decline the agent's offer to further service you and congratulate him or her for finding yet another opportunity to sell life insurance. Call several agents in your area to get annual premium costs for term insurance. If you erroneously believe that term insurance is too expensive at retirement, you would lose total consciousness if you saw the premiums for cash value insurance. If the insurance industry didn't so successfully pawn them off as investment vehicles, only the most uninformed consumers would even look at them. The term premium will be cheaper.

This is called pension maximation, and it is abused by insurance agents who convince you to purchase very expensive whole life or universal life or variable life insurance policies because they represent very large commission checks.

In general, the greater the lump sum, the more prudent to take it with you. You can work your money, watch it more closely, and probably create better returns. If you choose one of the monthly pension options, what will happen if your company flies South with the geese in a few years? Who will guarantee that the necessary monthly check will continue ?

What if your company goes belly up? You will have many retirement years to hope that it stays healthy. Time is a great risk factor. You are betting that your company will stay in business, but you are not sitting on the board of directors with a bird's eye view, inside information, and a golden parachute. These risks may be more important factors to consider than receiving a few more dollars of benefit each month.

If you choose one of the monthly payment options, you will find a discrepancy between the larger check on your life alone and the option where the company is taking a risk on two lives, yours and your spouse's.

A comfortable retirement takes more than money

While financial security cannot be over-emphasized, planning for retirement involves more than having sufficient income. Many retirees are uncertain how they will spend their time, while others plan specific goals, objectives and memories.

Although many workers can't wait to call their boss and tell them, "I'm not coming in today, or tomorrow, or any other day" (the civilized version of "take this job and shove it"), some workers may feel depressed, displaced and directionless. This happens especially when they have spent long years with one company or have become very involved with their jobs. The prospect of having to fill each day, seven days a week, with things *other* than work may be frightening.

Occasionally, when a spouse retires, he or she will seek greater attention from his or her partner. Even couples who care deeply about each other can have *too* much togetherness. Do not sacrifice your comfortable daily lifestyle to subordinate your activities to your partner. Eventually, you may resent your decision.

Remind your spouse that you care but have other interests. Suggest activities your spouse can explore. Avoid guilt or the feeling of intimidation. Perhaps you can set up special pre-scheduled combination activities for both of you to look forward to. Telling your partner on a regular basis to "get a life" or to "buzz off" is not going to solve the basic problem. Find a kinder, gentler way to get your message across.

There are many areas to evaluate as you plan various aspects of your retirement years. Evaluate your accomplishments. Assess your strengths and weaknesses. Think about your likes and dislikes. Visualize the activities you currently enjoy that can be expanded. Widen your personal and social interests. Explore new opportunities and pursuits. Think about new job opportunities (where the primary objective is personal satisfaction rather than the almighty paycheck). Volunteer projects, church work, travel, and taking good physical care of yourself are examples.

Experiment with new ideas. Develop new interests and friendships. During your working years, all output had a purpose, detailed structure, and ulcer-inducing deadlines. Now you can create your own life. You have greater freedom than ever before (providing the financial problems are minimal).

Don't discover too late that there is more to retirement than staying home from work.

Your Retirement Planning Checklist

1. Determine when you are eligible to retire.

2. Identify the factors that affect your pension computation.

3. Make a decision regarding the survivor election (different options available such as a lump sum, life income for you only, or life income for both you and your spouse).

4. Make decisions regarding health and death insurance.

5. Determine your Social Security benefits. (Send in a request for earnings now to compare benefits with our Tables and to check the accuracy of all earnings credits.)

6. Estimate your monthly retirement needs.

7. Determine the monthly retirement income needed.

8. Analyze your supplemental retirement savings plans.

9. Adjust your investment vehicles for comfort, not for speed.

10. Determine the monthly income shortfall (gap).

11. Calculate the annual savings necessary.

12. Apply for Social Security benefits three months before eligible.

13. Apply for Medicare Part A three months before age 65.

14. Evaluate whether to enroll in Medicare Part B.

15. Follow additional steps to prepare for and insure a comfortable retirement.

PORTFOLIO PLANNING WORKSHEET

Primary Investment Objective:_____

1. Cash, Checking Accounts, Emergency Funds, CDs

Where Deposited	Objective	$ Value	Percent of Portfolio
_____	_____	_____	_____
_____	_____	_____	_____
_____	_____	_____	_____
_____	_____	_____	_____
_____	_____	_____	_____
_____	_____	_____	_____
_____	_____	_____	_____
_____	_____	_____	_____
TOTAL		_____	__100.00%__

2. Retirement Programs, College Funding, Vehicles For Other Goals:

Name of Vehicle	Objective	$ Value	Percent of Portfolio
_____	_____	_____	_____
_____	_____	_____	_____
_____	_____	_____	_____

_____	_____	_____	_____
_____	_____	_____	_____
_____	_____	_____	_____
_____	_____	_____	_____
_____	_____	_____	_____
_____	_____	_____	_____
_____	_____	_____	_____

3. Regular Investment Programs (IRA, SEP, 401K, 403B, profit-sharing, ESOP, bonds):

Name of Vehicle	Amount of Investment	Frequency	Present Value
_____	_____	_____	_____
_____	_____	_____	_____
_____	_____	_____	_____
_____	_____	_____	_____
_____	_____	_____	_____
_____	_____	_____	_____
_____	_____	_____	_____
_____	_____	_____	_____
_____	_____	_____	_____
_____	_____	_____	_____

Total Compensation Benefits

1. Group Basic Term Life Insurance ❑ YES ❑ NO
    Amount _____

2. Optional Term or other Life Insurance ❑ YES ❑ NO
    Amount _____

3. Deferred Compensation ❑ YES ❑ NO
    Amount _____

4. Retirement Health Plan ❑ YES ❑ NO
    Amount _____

5. Retirement Insurance Plan ❑ YES ❑ NO
    Amount _____

6. Supplementary Retirement Savings ❑ YES ❑ NO

    Employer Match _____% ❑ YES ❑ NO

    Lump Sum Retirement Option ❑ YES ❑ NO
    (Such as 401k, ESOP, 403b, TSA)

7. Thrift Savings Plan ❑ YES ❑ NO

    Employer Match _____% ❑ YES ❑ NO

8. Spouse Health Retirement Plan ❑ YES ❑ NO

9. Special Considerations ❑ YES ❑ NO

Types of Survivor Elections

1. Lump Sum Pension Payment ❑ YES ❑ NO

2. Yourself Only Life Monthly Annuity ❑ YES ❑ NO

3. Former Spouse Survivor Annuity ❑ YES ❑ NO

4. Yourself/Spouse Survivor Annuity ❑ YES ❑ NO

5. Combination Current/Former Spouse ❑ YES ❑ NO

6. Special Pension Alternatives ❑ YES ❑ NO

7. Social Security Combination ❑ YES ❑ NO

Retirement Worksheet

1. Annual gross income needed at retirement (75% - 80% of current income in today's dollars, not adjusted for inflation) _____

2. Probable future Social Security benefits _____

3. Probable future company pension benefits _____
(If your company pension is integrated or combined with Social Security, complete only line 2 or 3, not both)

4. Add together line 2 and line 3 for total benefits _____

5. Annual retirement income needed from personal savings and investments (line 1 minus line 4) _____

6. Amount you must save before retirement (line 5 multiplied by Table A [page 111]) _____

7. Personal retirement savings already accumulated (this includes IRAs, annuities, 401ks not noted above, 403b or TSA plans, corporate savings plans, supplementary deferred compensation, company stock, or ESOPS, and miscellaneous investments earmarked for retirement needs.) _____

8. Projected future value of retirement savings at retirement time (line 7 multiplied by Table B [page 112]) _____

9. Amount of retirement capital still needed (line 6 minus line 8) _____

10. Annual savings needed to reach your goal (line 9 multiplied by Table C [page 112]) _____

11. Annual savings needed (line 10 minus annual employer contributions to retirement funds) _____

Sample Retirement Worksheet

1. Annual gross income needed at retirement (75% - 80% of current income in today's dollars, not adjusted for inflation) $40,000

2. Probable future Social Security benefits $12,000

3. Probable future company pension benefits $8,000
(If your company pension is integrated or combined with Social Security, complete only line 2 or 3, not both.)

4. Add together line 2 and line 3 for total benefits $20,000

5. Annual retirement income needed from personal savings and investments (line 1 minus line 4) $20,000

6. Amount you must save before retirement (line 5 multiplied by Table A [page 111]) $384,000

7. Personal retirement savings already accumulated $200,000

8. Projected future value of retirement savings at retirement time (line 7 multiplied by Table B [page 112]) $258,000

9. Amount of retirement capital still needed (line 6 minus line 8) $126,000

10. Annual savings needed to reach your goal (line 9 multiplied by Table C [page 112]) $12,474

11. Annual savings needed (line 10 minus annual employer contributions to retirement funds) $7,474

Projected Annual Social Security Benefits

(Top line is worker's current annual salary)

Worker's Current Age	$30,000	$40,000	$50,000	$51,300+
45 Worker	13,488	15,156	16,704	17,064
45 w/spouse	20,232	22,728	25,056	25,596
55 Worker	12,168	13,272	14,172	14,340
55 w/spouse	18,252	19,908	21,252	21,504
65 Worker	11,112	11,784	12,252	12,264
65 w/spouse	16,668	17,676	18,372	18,396

Source: Social Security Administration, 1991

Table A

Age at Retirement	Retirement Factor A
55	23.3
56	22.9
57	22.6
58	22.2
59	21.8
60	21.4
61	21.0
62	20.5
63	20.1
64	19.6
65	19.2
66	18.7
67	18.2

Table B

Years to Retirement	Retirement Factor B
5	1.15
7	1.22
9	1.29
11	1.36
13	1.44
15	1.53
20	1.76
25	2.02
30	2.33

Table C

Years to Retirement	Retirement Factor C
5	0.188
7	0.131
9	0.099
11	0.079
13	0.065
15	0.054
20	0.038
25	0.028
30	0.022

The factors used in these worksheets assume a hypothetical 8% before-tax return and a 5% inflation rate. They are only to be used as a general guideline. Always consult your tax advisor before making major financial decisions.

Chapter 11

The Last Frontier: College Funding

One of the most serious challenges facing parents today is college funding, and it usually smacks them in the pocketbook one or two years before high school graduation. That is not enough time to accumulate the major dollars needed, and panic management, borrowing, and a lot of "we're doing it for the kids, Ethel" help most parents endure and survive those college years. My sympathies to those parents with more than one dependent to educate.

By the time your love child heads off for the Ivy-covered walls, you will have chauffeured him or her approximately 145,000 miles—nearly to the moon—without ever receiving one Frequent Flyer award. You will cut, paste, paint, glue, hold, blow dry and repair more Scout, 4-H, Junior Achievement, and school Science Fair projects than you ever thought one child could possibly enroll in. You will wonder when they have the class time to learn how to read designer labels and calculate allowance money.

The older your child gets, the more menial and minimum-wage type tasks he or she will need from you—car driving, button sewing, jeans washing, message taking, refrigerator closing, forgotten-thing delivering, broken heart listening, drain unclogging, and zit checking.

You will, I am happy to assure you, successfully emerge from the temporary driver license phase, the first boy/girl crush, and the pimple stage. You will think you have been through it all—until you arrive at the Fall high school financial aid meeting for parents of college-bound students, more commonly known to survivors as the "Do I look like a Savings and Loan?" phase.

This is as good a time as any to buy your personal bumper sticker that will keep you going through four or even more years of hamburger surprise, macaroni and whatever-is-left-over, and gluing together the soles of your shoes one more time: Get Revenge. Live Long Enough To Become A Burden To Your Children.

Make a new plan, Stan

Surviving the college years is the ultimate test of good long-term planning, self-sacrifice, and, perhaps, your sanity. Parents ask me when it will ever end. Hopefully, before you have mortgaged everything you own...and your future to boot.

The ideal time to start planning for your child's college education is the day your baby is born. The best gift young parents can give to their pink or blue bundle is the promise of at least $25 per month set up in an automatic investment plan. Even with eighteen years for these systematic payments to compound, this will fall short of the average cost of a four-year public university education. But it *will* lop off between $15,000 and $20,000 of the amount you need to raise.

How much should you save each month or each year to be ready? Fortunately, there are definite answers. Most folks are taught to set goals by throwing some funding at financial products, crossing their fingers, closing their eyes to the continuing problem, and hoping that somehow things will turn out. You need accurate projections.

If you have plenty of years left until matriculation time, use the charts and worksheets later in this chapter to get you focused on both the problem and the solution.

If you were hoping that this chapter would provide the miracle cure for *next* year's college freshman, you will need to look through these last-minute options:

1. Home equity loans
2. National Direct Student (Perkins) Loans (NDSLS)[1]

3. Guaranteed Student (Stafford) Loans[2]
4. Supplemental Loans for Students
5. Parent Loans to Undergraduate Students (PLUS)[3]
6. Borrowing against life insurance values
7. Refinancing a home mortgage
8. Retirement plan loans
9. Retirement plan termination
10. Military programs
11. Loans against portfolio securities
12. Cooperative education
13. Company-sponsored education
14. Community college commuting

[1] Need-based, low-interest loans made through a school's financial aid office.
[2] Low-interest government loans offered by banks, savings and loans, or credit unions.
[3] Made through banks, savings and loans, or credit unions.

If college is around the corner

If college is within two years, your investment options are limited. This short-term goal comes under the heading of "short-term money." The appropriate vehicles are spelled out later in this book.

For short-term investing, stick with investment vehicles without sales charges, surrender charges, annual fees, or other distribution or heavy management expenses. It doesn't take a rocket scientist to manage a U.S. Government money market mutual fund or to sign you up for a bank CD. With little time left, safety of principal is your first priority.

If you have the time

If your education funding goal is longer than three years from today, completely different funding strategies will be appropriate. Your primary goal with such long-term money must be conservation of purchasing power, not safety first.

The strategies for long-term money discussed later in this book should be examined. Working against your long-term education goal, inflation will loom as your worst enemy, loss of principal as your secondary adversary, and procrastination as the third common reason for failure in this area.

No matter how much you save, you are in for one rude awakening. Essentially, the more responsibly you lead your life, the more you will be penalized by receiving little or no financial aid for your child's college education.

(There are other suggestions as well as good basic college planning advice in my first book, *Get Rich Slow*. It is worth getting for this chapter alone, because it discusses the pros and cons of all the options at your command and presents a basic planning guide for parents willing to sacrifice their self-interest to provide their children with the tools desperately needed in today's economy. That chapter should also be read by every teenager who doesn't want his or her parents to retire as wards of the state and go bankrupt in the process.)

Pre-paid college tuition plans

The Sizzle: States as well as colleges and universities are feeling the pressure to address the serious problem of funding current costs, and several have instituted pre-paid programs to tackle the onslaught of inflation and the escalating costs of private and public schools.

Under most pre-paid tuition plans, a parent or grand-parent (or any other benefactor) can contribute current payments which will guarantee a certain number of future credits toward tuition. For example a parent can make sufficient payments to guarantee one, two, three, or even all four years of college credits that will fund the tuition bill when the child becomes college bound, no matter how much of a toll inflation takes on costs in 5, 10, 15, or even 18 years.

The college, university, or state usually holds this money in a trust which invests the pool into various conservative investment instruments. The parent or benefactor receives confirmation of the guaranteed future college education credits. Pre-paid plans are particularly appealing due to the school's or state's guarantee that *no matter how much college costs escalate,* your pre-paid tuition payments today will stretch into the next century and provide the same relative amount of education that they do today.

The Steak: Though these sound admirable and offer a well-meaning and safe harbor for parents to run to, in most states they have not worked well and have been discontinued. To understand the difference between intentions and results, let's analyze the promises that are made by these state programs (or specific college programs).

They offer cost guarantees in spite of any projected inflation increases. At present, college costs are inching upward yearly by 6%-10%, with the latter figure being more common. Any guaranteed fiduciary fund (the fund of all the prepaid tuitions the college receives) would have to be invested in conservative (I mean *really* conservative) things like CDs or U.S. Government bills or notes. When we discussed inflationary pressures, we learned that it wasn't what we made on our money that counted, it was what we made after inflation that really mattered. It is currently impossible to receive an overall *before*-inflation rate of return of even 8% from those investments. Those investment vehicles are strictly for short-term needs or for those who need income above all else.

Where are the states or colleges going to invest your money to achieve an 8%-10% rate of return *after* inflation, without taking too much risk? ***Nowhere.***

(We haven't even considered the costs of maintaining such a fund pool—clerical and administrative bills plus costs of some fiduciary management group plus brokerage fees for buying and selling within the trust account, paying for all of which will require an even *greater* return.)

Conclusion: It is impossible for anyone to "safely" invest your dollars today and keep pace with inflation over the years.

Any such trust fund with inflation guarantees will have to venture out further into risk territory, picking from the basket of stocks, bonds, real estate, etc. None of the above are safe from loss of principal. All will move up and down with their respective markets. So much for the safety of principal *and* inflation guarantees. The bold print can advertise it, but the fine print may have to take it away if some of the assets have done poorly when you need to turn the tuition spigot into dollars. A paper guarantee won't send your child to school. Only sufficient dollars will.

What if your child doesn't go to college? When can you get your money back? What if he or she goes to an out-of-state school? When does your money come back to you? What if you need your money in the meantime? Once you have given the money to them, you have lost all future control. Individual sums usually cannot be redeemed at a parent's request.

What if the trust suffers enough losses next year (or in 5 years) so that it will have to make even greater returns in the future to guarantee its future promises? Will it have to accept even greater risk in an effort to recover its losses? What accountants will be watching day and night for mismanagement or inappropriate activity? Whether you realize it or not, most plans have their own escape clauses in case of adverse circumstances. Where are yours?

The Bottom Line: On the whole, these programs are well-intentioned attempts to help parents provide their children with an affordable education. But, when we start asking tough questions and working our pencils, we find holes big enough to drive a truck through.

A guarantee is only as good in the end as the company or group backing it up. "Sorry, we tried" won't help when you march your child up the steps to Ivy U with your handwritten excuse. The school will want a tuition check instead.

A far better method of "guaranteeing" your child's education is to take charge of your own pre-paid tuition plan. Invest your money in a conservative mutual fund and add to it on a systematic monthly basis over the years. You will receive a higher rate of return, have fewer costs associated with its management, exercise more control over the principal, and gain some tax relief by labeling it as a Uniform Gift to Minors

Account (UGMA). (In a UMGA the child legally owns the money, has an adult custodian overseeing all investment decisions until the child is age 18, and enjoys favorable tax advantages. You, as the custodian, can watch it, change its direction, and use the money for other needs of your child if necessary.)

Use the worksheets on the following pages to learn how much *you* need to save to give your child the education you'd like (or can afford) to.

College Funding Worksheet

STEP 1: Estimating the cost of a college education

In column 1, enter your child's name and age. In column 2, enter the estimated annual cost for tuition, fees, room and board, and incidentals at whatever institution you are considering. (Sending for recent college catalogs of specific schools and universities can give you a rough estimate. For a broad overview, assume $7,000 for public institutions and $15,500 for a private institution...per year.)

Next, look up the Inflation Factor (according to your child's age) on the chart on page 121 and write that number in Column 3. Multiply the numbers in columns 2 and 3; write this answer in Column 4.

This number approximates what your child's four-year college education will cost.

Column 1	Column 2	Column 3	Column 4
_____	_____	_____	_____
_____	_____	_____	_____
_____	_____	_____	_____
_____	_____	_____	_____
_____	_____	_____	_____

STEP 2: Estimating the Annual Savings Required

In column 1, enter your child's name and age. In column 2, enter the estimated total future costs from Step 1. Find the Savings Factor from the chart on page 121 and enter that figure in Column 3. Multiply the numbers in columns 2 and 3; write your answer in column 4.

***This number is the amount you have to save each year—
starting now—to accumulate sufficient money for the college
you have chosen.***

Column 1	Column 2	Column 3	Column 4
_____	_____	_____	_____
_____	_____	_____	_____
_____	_____	_____	_____
_____	_____	_____	_____
_____	_____	_____	_____

Inflation Factor/Savings Factor Chart

Child's Age	Inflation Factor	Savings Factor
1	11.780	0.025
2	11.113	0.027
3	10.484	0.031
4	9.891	0.034
5	9.331	0.038
6	8.803	0.043
7	8.304	0.049
8	7.834	0.056
9	7.391	0.064
10	6.972	0.074
11	6.578	0.087
12	6.205	0.104
13	5.854	0.126
14	5.523	0.158
15	5.210	0.205
16	4.915	0.285
17	4.637	0.445
18	4.375	0.926

Note: The above inflation factor assumes an annual rate of return of 8%.

Chapter 12

Where's *Your* Piggy Bank?

We are a good natured bunch of saps in this country.
When the market drops 50 points, we are supposed not to
know it's manipulation.
When a bank fails, we let the guy go start another one.
—Will Rogers

The great bank holdup.. just happened

Every version detailing the Savings and Loan industry's
woes is different. One thing is for sure: No one warned the
taxpayer to get out of the way. Whether the result of greed,
criminal activity, or mismanagement of assets coupled with
an unfriendly market, this shameful cleanup bill has been
sent to the consumer.

Piggy bank

Thrifts made money during the 1980s, though they
screamed about nearly every administrative policy Washington and the Federal Reserve fostered. Perhaps no one knew
what else to do. Maybe it seemed reasonable that Savings and
Loans be allowed to outgrow the thin financial ice they stood
on. Maybe everyone (including Wall Street) was making so
much money off lending activity that no one cared.
It is common knowledge (and common sense) that whenever you give the private sector (or the government sector) a
safety net (FDIC), they immediately practice highwire balancing acts. Somehow prudence flies out the window.

This little piggy went to market

The Federal Reserve (the Fed) determines directly or indirectly what banks will pay for borrowing money (the discount rate), what banks charge their best customers (the prime), and what the banks must pay into the FDIC kitty for reserve requirements.

You are not a bank borrowing overnight extra reserves, nor one of their best customers. You are merely a customer, the kind that banks depend on when no bigwheels are hanging around to borrow shovelfuls of money. You are the little guy who can buy only one house at a time and only two cars to a paycheck.

Without you banks have no money to loan, but since no one reminds you how indispensable you are, you still are intimidated when entering the local shrine where they keep the big vaults and (supposedly) the large piles of dollars.

When the Fed needs to stimulate the economy, it can lower the interest rates banks must pay for reserves, and assumes that the lenders will then lower their rates to all bank customers because they will still make a decent profit spread.

But nobody explained these rules to the bankers. When the Fed reduced the discount rate, bankers rejoiced because their costs had gone down. It never occurred to them to pass these savings to their customers. Why, that would shave off some profits!

So CDs and savings accounts started their descent, a little at a time, not so much that you would notice (unless you were watching). Every time the Fed acted, bankers ran to their rate signs and adjusted the numbers downward on customer deposits.

They did not, however, decrease the cost of consumer borrowing to any great extent like the public thought they had. In fact, in some areas like credit card debt (where they had a captive audience) they even *increased* the annual percentage rates. Knowing that consumers could not pay off balances until their paychecks got larger, lenders could charge almost anything they wanted to.

This little piggy stayed home

Instead of actually reducing mortgage rates, car loans, home equity loans, or credit card interest, they just advertised that they had. They would mark down the mortgage rate a bit but then jack up the points and closing costs enough to offset the decrease in the mortgage interest. Realizing that most folks couldn't pay the points up front, they would roll those into the re-financed mortgage or thirty-year indentured servant plan, and the banks would make interest on higher points and closing costs for many years.

Bankers confided in me that it would be ludicrous to actually bring interest rates down when the public already thought they had. Why have a sale when the merchandise was selling like hotcakes without one?

Bankers are agreed on this stance: If the recession is to be solved, it will certainly not be on the backs of the banking industry. Everyone can just go find some other ox to gore. And if we don't shoo away soon, they might lower the CD rate again, just for spite.

After all, there is little profit in banking these days. Bankers mainly do this because they like to be around people. They don't need this consumer hostility. So we had better stop bothering them so they can get back to counting dollars in their backrooms.

Banks don't really want to loan out a lot of money right now. So they don't want to pay you a lot for it while it gathers dust around the neighborhood branch. It's the same principle that other suppliers follow today—"just in time" delivery. It costs to keep inventory on hand that isn't going out one door as fast as it is coming in. So companies can cut costs by ordering what they need, but only at the last minute.

It is not feasible for your local bank to send a courier around the neighborhood calling for deposits because they have a customer sitting at the loan desk, waiting for a pickup. So it will take in your money now and attempt to cut its costs by decreasing your interest rate until the dollars are bought (loaned out).

I don't get no respect

Rodney Dangerfield made this line famous, but there are millions of Rodneys firmly ensconced in passbook savings accounts paying less than fish food rates, while these same consumers complain about rising inflation or worry when the Social Security check is late, vehemently maligning doctors and others for charging escalating fees.

Banks haven't really competed for your dollars for years. They didn't have to. They sat in neighborhood shopping malls and at the end of your street waiting for you to drop by for the sake of convenience. You demanded convenience, not rate of return. You had better things to do with your valuable time.

There is a place for some bank CDs in your total portfolio. Now that S&Ls and commercial banks are both backed by the promises of the FDIC, it makes little difference whether you patronize one or the other even if you believe one type is safer than the other. The recent lending crisis wasn't just isolated to S&Ls. Generally, S&Ls can offer higher time deposit returns than their commercial counterparts.

It probably is not wise to loan all your time deposits to just one institution. If there should be a liquidity problem due to a bank failure, or some future individual insolvencies, you can feel less concerned by diversifying your Certificates of Deposit. I am betting (your money) that more than one lender at a time won't get into trouble. Don't let your greed factor convince you to leave all your eggs inside one basket.

You must always be watchful, no matter where you invest. You must listen carefully to everything you hear. Cats are well-known for selective hearing when their owners scold. But you must understand the meaning of every word you are told.

This little piggy now has roast beef

In formulating a survival defense in this low-return market, many banks have entered the insurance industry business with insurance fixed annuities and other CD-like investments. The sleight-of-hand here is the term "CD-like." No CD-like investment is backed by the Federal Deposit Insurance Corporation (FDIC). This is marketing hype.

Here's the kind of sales pitch to look out for:

> "We are _____, and although we're not *really* the Bank, we are very closely *associated* with the Bank, and maybe even *owned* by the Bank. We would like to show you *our* CD alternative we sell right here *in the bank building*. Now, it is not insured by the FDIC, but we have *really* researched this and feel that this company is *very safe* for your money or we *certainly* wouldn't be showing it to you.
>
> "It has a *much* higher return than the Bank can give you, and look at all this *tax-free* income you'll accumulate every year until you take it out. And if you never take it out, the money will keep compounding *tax-free* until it goes to your heirs, outside that awful thing called probate.
>
> "You certainly qualify for tax relief plus the higher interest rate.
>
> "The choice is up to you, and we certainly don't want to push you into anything. We *especially* don't want to push you into the bank's low-yielding, *taxable* CDs."

Most customers are going to remember three things from this pitch: safe, high-yield, and tax-free. That's enough. Wrap it up. Take it home.

Instead of salivating at a modestly higher yield, bells should be clanging. Why is the bank suggesting you send your money anywhere else? Isn't the manager's primary job to keep your money *there?* What is the motive for this sudden change of heart?

If solicited in this manner, suggest that your banker stop imagining you are so naive that this deception might work. And tell the manager that as soon as your current CD matures, you will be off to the bank down the street.

There is a large insurance industry crisis brewing, in case your insurance agent hasn't notified you. This is no time to be taking a leap of insolvency faith. At least wait until this insurance uncertainty blows over and you can identify the survivors. For now stick to 12-month CDs and keep moving them to whichever lender shows you the most respect. If banks really want to compete for your dollars, I have a suggestion: try raising the CD rates.

Timing is everything

Instead of guessing at future interest rates where you will be either 100% correct or 100% incorrect, you can purchase some insurance either way the interest market moves. During times when longer deposits mean significantly higher yields, put half of your CD money into 1-year CDs, the other half into 18-month or 2-year CD deposits. Make your choice depending on the attractiveness of the yield differentials over longer time periods.

Don't lock in longer rates for a small incremental rise. Make lenders coax you into longer terms with substantially increased rates.

After the first twelve months, you will have a re-investment decision, but only on half of your CD assets. If interest rates have gone up, you can move to higher yields on half of your money. If they have declined, at least half your money will still be locked in and working at higher rates for another six months.

I would not sweat over any decision to lengthen my deposit more than two years for anything under a 9% yield.

Call several institutions and compare their CD rates. Be careful. Marketing CDs has become a profitable pastime of some bankers. CD advertisements can be so complex that they are deceiving. Is a 5.8% for 6 months, then 6.5% for 6 months, and a 7.2% for the last 6 months of an 18-month CD better than an overall 6.5% for 18 months?

You can't easily compute rates without a compound interest calculator. But when you request the annual effective return, you are putting all the CDs on an equal basis. Another method of comparing is to ask if you give them your money, how much will be in your account at the end of the year?

Secret CD and IRA rollovers

Some banking institutions are less than forthright communicating maturity dates with you. Some will openly send you a letter stating your withdrawal rights, while others will silently hope you don't remember your original IRA statement date until the 7-day maturity withdrawal period has safely passed.

You do have some rights in this matter. First, you have 14 days to tell your banker that this tactic is sleazy and didn't work, and that you are taking your money now that you can plainly see how they practice banking. If you have already passed your grace period, you should scream loudly on Saturday morning in the crowded institution that your money has been kidnapped until someone in power offers to shut you up by releasing your funds with apologies that they really thought you meant to leave it there on your own recognizance.

The old gray mare

Bank Money Market Demand Accounts (MMDAs) provide you with instant accessibility to your money or to certain withdrawal privileges at certain times during the month. Most bankers don't like this "hot money" and price their MMDAs unattractively. This lower rate encourages customers to choose other bank instruments the institution can better utilize for its own profit purposes.

Don't confuse bank Money Market Accounts with the money market mutual funds that have become so popular. Bank Money Market Demand Accounts are insured by the FDIC, but you certainly pay heavily for the protection—a lower yield. Consider comparing with U.S. Government Agency money market mutual funds and use only what you need for liquidity for either kind of account.

Short stop money

Though we should maximize returns on all our dollars, short-term money must be deposited first with safety of principal in mind, yield a secondary factor. Therefore, you are going to sacrifice some return to get the safety of principal. Short-term dollars are those which must be utilized by you within a two to three-year period. Use only a combination of CDs and money market instruments (U.S. Government money market mutual funds). Brokerages and other financial institutions may lure you with promises of higher yields. Stay where you are. Higher yield means higher risk of principal. If your time horizon is so short, what will you do if the product's underlying securities turn against you?

The foundation of your investment portfolio could consist of the following types of securities and bank products:

1. Interest-bearing checking account for everyday purchases and monthly bills;
2. A money market U.S. Government mutual fund for larger but liquid cash assets and check-writing privileges;
3. 1-year Certificates of Deposit (only FDIC insured);
4. 18-month or 2-year Certificates of Deposit (when higher interest rates warrant the longer lock-ins).

This foundation is your security blanket. We will discuss the remainder of your investment portfolio and inflation-fighting vehicles in the following chapter on long-term money.

As safe as money in the bank

Not all CDs are created equal. You need to ask if your CD will be insured by the FDIC. Though no one will lie regarding this important difference, some vendors may not volunteer this pertinent information.

There are private corporations who create what they call Certificates. They are *not* the same. These are *not* insured by the FDIC and are only backed by the private companies issuing them. That single difference is large enough to warrant wondering whether any extra yield is worth the increased risk. If a private corporation becomes insolvent, declares bankruptcy, or otherwise goes into default, you will be an unsecured creditor, waiting either for assets to be released or for something leftover after the company liquidation.

Usually, there is no secured property like a building or equipment for you to confiscate. (Senior debtors have already spoken for those items.) You may be posed on a long list of general creditors if sufficient assets are ever available.

A higher yield is a clue that the Certificate may only have private company backing. Some banks have sold these Certificates backed only by private bank assets of the institution. If these default (and some of them have), it is possible to lose all of your money. Always ask if the Certificate you are being offered is insured, and insured by the Federal Deposit Insurance Corporation.

Package banking

To catch a mouse, one must make a noise like a cheese. Banks offer all types of advantaged banking services and wrap programs to attract seniors, young adults, newly married couples, and parents. From interest-bearing (NOW) checking accounts along with minimum savings or CD specifications, money market demand accounts, low-cost checking and free minimum balance checking accounts, to jumbo CD rates and membership in a club which offers a variety of extra services, bank products are coming into the 1990s as heavily marketed as any other consumer product. (Personally, I would rather have better CD returns and fewer privileges. Evidently the privileges are cheaper for the institutions to offer.)

Watch for new user fees on accounts below certain levels, on check-writing accounts, on ATM cash withdrawals, and other freebies you once took for granted. Once a year, add up all the costs for your banking needs and compare with other local institutions. Comparison shop for *everything,* not just CD rates.

Be careful to calculate how much interest you are losing by signing up for packages that demand minimum account balances. These may look attractive on the surface, but you will be earning less on your savings than somewhere else, such as a money market mutual fund. How much will you save in fees and how much will you lose in opportunity costs?

With free lunches, always be cautious. Account services for those over age 50 or age 55 are very popular. Read the fine print and know what you may be giving up in opportunity costs of investing somewhere else. Some banks advertise club memberships and charge one monthly charge for several service options. Compare with your individual needs. Packages aren't always better deals. Be sure you will use those privileges enough to make the service profitable for you. If you write few checks and don't need travelers checks or notary services, you may not receive the value you paid for.

Ho, ho, ho, humbug!

Christmas Clubs are also popular, yet the worst performing interest accounts you can join, even with the free lunch of one free payment at the holidays. Even so, I occasionally recommend them because, in spite of their poor economic value, they can at least make Christmas a cash transaction rather than a credit card statement with payments stretching until next June.

Bank IRAs and retirement fund rollovers

IRAs (Individual Retirement Accounts) are considered long-term money, and retirement money sitting in Certificates of Deposit (FDIC insured or not) will not outpace inflation over the years. There are losses other than loss of principal. This problem is highlighted by many elderly who never knew any investment vehicles but their neighborhood banking system.

Lenders are to be congratulated for the positive effect they had on the IRA. They advertised the devil out of them. But they certainly never told customers that they might find a better one down the street. IRA money must maintain purchasing power over conservation of principal. So you need to look at alternative investment vehicles for at least part of your IRA funds, such as conservative mutual funds.

Maybe you *should* leave home without it

Lending institutions offer major credit cards such as VISA and Mastercard. Each lender has a unique and specific agreement for its particular credit card. Therefore, interest rates and terms may vary significantly. Shop for the best credit card on a national basis, and resist buying one from your lender through their solicitation.

If you are truly using "OPM" (Other People's Money) wisely, you are borrowing the lender's money free each month during the grace period and paying off your credit card balance *in full* each month. Search for a credit card with no annual fee.

If, however, you use a credit card on the installment plan through a series of monthly payments when you charge, forget how much you will save with no annual fee and concentrate on finding the lowest annual percentage rate (the lowest cost for borrowing money.)

Banks usually perform better in one specialty or another. So your best CD bank may not have the lowest credit card available. Consider this a separate part of your financial life.

Personal loans can often be cheaper through credit unions or other preferred lenders you may have membership with. When shopping for personal loan money, request the compound annual percentage interest (the annual effective yield on your borrowed amount), not just the simple interest figure.

How solvent is your lender?

Several private companies offer, for a fee, their ratings of lenders nationwide. This compendium is the "Who's Who" of the banking world. While you may feel more comfortable knowing that someone else thinks a lot of your banking institution, these are only opinions, charts, accounting ledgers, financial statements, and other rations. The banking industry can change quickly.

I recommend that clients keep their CDs close by, in their local geographical counties. Rumors will spread more quickly regarding possible insolvency. So you can hear gossip quicker if your CD holder is close by.

People are so eager for reassurance that they will purchase unnecessary publications which promise peace of mind. The best inside information comes from leaks inside the institutions, not necessarily from outside sources peeking in. Your lender simply cannot tell you if your bank is in financial trouble because that would threaten a run on the bank. So you are left with whatever information you can dig up. If you do hear rumors, consider moving your assets unless you face severe penalties on deposits. Better safe than sorry.

Most of us realize our money isn't gathering dust in the vault. It has been loaned out to citizens based on the confidence of their ability to keep monthly mortgage payments and interest flowing back into the bank in a timely fashion. During a recession, pressure on lenders becomes greater. Less solvent institutions may offer better yields to attract dollars and improve their financial positions. You must balance the greed factor, the promises of the FDIC, and the potential feeling in the pit of your stomach should you hear on the evening news that tomorrow will be sunny but your lending institution is taking a short vacation.

Giving out final grades

When you move from lender to lender for better interest rates, you should let the former know why you are leaving. This can become leverage and food for thought as your message is passed upstairs to top management. Explain to your manager that you will be glad to come back when they show you greater respect—and you define respect as extra dollars in your pocketbook.

You have no right to complain about someone stealing your living room sofa if you left it sitting overnight on the front curb. If you play victim, you will find those willing to accommodate. Stop laying on the double yellow lines in the middle of the highway and start demanding these institutions make money the old-fashioned way—by competing for it and working hard, like you do for your paycheck.

Chapter 13

Using Your Kids
for a Change

A married couple planning a family today will spend approximately $150,0000 to raise that child to age eighteen. Another $100,000 to $150,000 to educate him or her in a public college or university.

Let's face it: Children are economic disasters.

They do eventually leave and live (mostly) off their own paychecks. But in the meantime, you may need to sell blood on a monthly basis to afford to keep them. The standard dependent deduction is a joke and a cruel reminder, considering their actual cost. Today's hospital maternity bills should be a cue to what comes later.

Before 1986, children and tax relief were a better partnership. Called income shifting or income splitting, it was relatively easy to gift or otherwise transfer assets to your children and have the profits taxed at their lower tax rates, or even excluded (tax-free) in some cases. It was even legal to take back the principal after ten years. Gift transfer and estate tax advantages were plentiful.

Then tax reform gutted many previous income and earnings shelters.

Kids may still be less taxing

There are still many avenues for getting revenge and reducing the drain of financial resources to them. The Kiddie Tax is here, and the child's ability to claim an additional personal exemption if the parent claimed him or her as a dependent is gone.

But there is still a long list of options blessed by the IRS. Always consider tax planning in light of other criteria. If you have a child who is already threatening to sue each time you enforce bedtime rules, some of these are definitely not for you. (Though a brochure telling you the earliest age the French Foreign Legion inducts members may be appropriate.)

Gifts to minors under age 14

Since the Kiddie Tax applies only to children under age 14, you can control somewhat which child will fit most efficiently under this strategy. Gifts of property producing unearned income—investments such as dividends and interest—of up to $550 per year are not taxed to anyone, even the child. In other words, if the child has no earned income (the kind that comes from real w-o-r-k), each year he or she can earn $550 from investments tax-free and never have to pay taxes to the IRS.

The next $550 of profits per year are taxed at the child's marginal (top) rate, probably 15%, usually lower than that of the parents. So on the first $1,100 of unearned income, the total tax per year will equal $82.50, a far cry from $308 if taxed at the parent's federal 28% marginal tax bracket (or $341 at a 31% federal tax bracket).

Any excess profits of unearned income over $1,100 will be shifted to the parents and taxed at their highest rate, usually 28% or 31%.

Gifts to minors age 14 or older

The Kiddie Tax disappears and the first $550 of profit is not taxed at all, while any excess over the $550 of unearned income is taxed at the child's lower rate, no matter how much profit has been made. This potentially saves 16% federal taxes from the highest marginal 31% adult tax bracket and 13% if the parent remains in the 28% marginal federal tax liability bracket. To summarize, no tax on the first $550 of profit and 15% on all excess profits above that amount of unearned income.

The gift to the child can qualify under the $10,000 gift tax exclusion. Currently, it is the business of the IRS if you should give your children your assets (before or after you are dead). Be careful you don't overgift and run afoul of the legal limits of generosity. Each parent can give $10,000 per year to each child (or your financial planner or favorite author)—a total of $20,000 per couple—without having to worry about being hit with a gift tax for giving too much to your children and none to the government.

This is an ideal way to fund college for your child and reduce your tax liability at the same time, or to start reducing your estate after retirement (if you are sure you won't later need the money for your own needs).

There are disadvantages to this seemingly wonderful strategy. Not all parents want their children to own large piles of assets while they are growing up. When you make a complete gift, you can't be an Indian giver. The money belongs to the *child,* though you can, in some cases, direct or control this money until he or she reaches the age of majority (18 or 21 depending on state statute).

Children tend to say and think nasty things to and about parents, and you have to know your child before you can feel comfortable legally giving them money while they are in their formative *(aka* Frankenstein) years.

Gifts from grandparents are also eligible. In other words, if the kids play it right, they can clean up from all their relatives—$10,000 per victim *per year.*

The simplest type of gift is an outright one. Confer with your accountant (preferably over lunch so you can get free advice) about the reporting of cash and/or property gifts. They are treated differently for tax reporting.

Custodial gifts

The Uniform Gift to Minors Act (and its expanded Uniform Transfers to Minors Act—UGMA or UTMA) legally gives the money to the child but retains the direction and control in the hands of an adult custodian. One custodian to each account, thank you. But the child could have many accounts, each with a different custodian. Depending on what your state will allow, more than cash or securities can fit. Perhaps pieces of real property and business interests can also be transferred.

If the parent acts as custodian and predeceases the child's age of majority (legal age of adulthood), the assets will be considered in the gross estate of the parent, though the child legally has ownership of the money. You can consider someone else as adult custodian to avoid this problem. But you, as the parents, are giving up the directional control of the money. Every time I give you the good news, I follow it up with some bad news. Sorry. Nothing is perfect. Weigh the advantages and problems on this issue.

The UGMA or UTMA has lots of flexibility. You, as a custodian, can direct the assets, change their investment structure, and use the money for the needs of the child, other than the basic survival responsibilities that any parent would shoulder. You should not take a trip to the Bahamas, purchase a new car with it, or attempt to convince your six-year-old that a 25-foot cabin cruiser would make a great Christmas present for the family. You must use it solely for the purpose of the child whose name is on the account. Unusual costs such as medical expenses are allowed.

I have received numerous inquiries as to whether a parent's psychiatrist fees are deductible during the teenage years since they are solely attributable to the child. This is pushing it. It is better to start your own mental health fund while the child is still small and have it available in your own name if needed. The child's transportation expenses to visit you at the sanitarium, however, are fully allowable.

U.S. Savings Bonds

These are widely used for gifts to children. On a long-term basis, I don't recommend them for accumulating assets for college or other financial goals because they don't keep pace with the inflationary and spiraling costs of college, even with the new tax gimmick. But our government keeps sugar-coating them because they are competing with every other financial vendor in the marketplace for your dollars.

If the child is under age 14 and has excess unearned income, the tax-deferred option of U.S. Savings bonds can be utilized—tax would not be due until sale of the bond. If there is little unearned income, perhaps it would be better to file taxes annually and, therefore, qualify for the $550 profit tax-free option.

State and local income taxes are not paid on these types of bonds. Have your accountant look at both options. Once you decide to pay taxes annually, you have burned the other tax bridge. This should not be a tough decision because you should be funding college education with growth vehicles, not government bonds. So you should only have a few of these to be concerned with.

U.S. Savings Bonds issued after 1989 are eligible for college tuition and expense tax-exempt status as the result of TAMRA 1988. This education-minded administration is offering these as a means of helping parents save for college and receive tax benefits. The government is helping itself to some benefits—the use of your money until you actually use it.

You can exclude from income (not count for taxes) all or part of the interest you receive from cashing your bond in the year it is redeemed for college tuition and related expenses (not for room and board or football team expenses). The bond must be a Series EE issued after December 31, 1989, in your name or that of your spouse (no grandparents allowed). You must be 24 years of age or older before the bond was issued.

Most public and private non-profit universities and colleges are eligible. Some vocational training schools also qualify. You can only redeem sufficient dollars to meet the eligible education expenses for the year or only part of the interest will be tax-free. The tax-free exclusion is also affected and reduced by any tax-free scholarships or other benefits received during the year. No *carte blanche* here.

If you make too much money at the time of redemption, according to the government (certainly not according to your figures)—over $90,000 for married couples filing together and $55,000 for all others—you will not qualify for this perk.

Son, you're hired

If you think you can stand more closeness than already exists, you can hire your child to do simple clerical, janitorial, or miscellaneous work. This benefit is sometimes abused, and your child should not be on vacation in the Galapagos Islands when he or she is supposedly working to earn money from your business. He or she must also be paid normal labor wages for the job being done.

There can be minor problems and potential expenses. If your teenager joins your home construction or clerical crew, Workman's Compensation, payroll taxes, unemployment taxes, and other expenses may be applicable. Your accountant can be responsible for examining if this arrangement would still be profitable for you. The Social Security tax (FICA) does not have to be paid on a child under age 18. This makes the choice of hiring your spouse over your children less palatable. Your spouse must now be counted for Social Security taxes (FICA).

The standard deduction (the total amount the child can earn and still avoid paying taxes) is $3,400 (in 1991). All amounts above that are subject to taxes at the child's rate. Of course, he can take his or her own dependent exemption, but you can probably use that better at your current tax bracket. Only one to a customer today. (The parents can continue to claim the child as a dependent as long as they contribute more than half of the child's support.)

Gifting securities

If you choose, you may consider gifting to your child appreciated (it made a profit) stock. The tax strategy here is to buy something that produces little income (such as dividends like AT&T) and majors in growth (like IBM used to). Of course, the major flaw in this theory is that going for the tax strategy first will result in your purchasing a riskier investment. Personally, I would give up some tax advantage to get better quality long-term stock.

Until college, the stock is owned by your child. Before Freshman week, the child sells the security and pays the taxes in a lower bracket, probably 15% instead of at your higher tax rate.

Of mice and men and child landlords

There is a great current interest in funding college primarily on the real estate ability of your college student— buying a property near campus, converting it to a rental (with depreciation benefits), and paying your child to take on all responsibilities, for which you can get a deduction and they can be paid, including negotiating student rentals for four years, maintaining basic custodian work, and generally watching the property for Mom and Dad. After graduation, parents can sell the house, pay some income taxes on the gain, and, if sold at a loss, recognize only the sale as a rental property. This has been recommended by some (so-called money gurus) as a great method of paying for a college education. The tuition comes from the monthly rental incomes of other students.

My translation of this Cinderella story is a bit different. The normal 18-year-old is hardly equipped to negotiate with other, taller and more intimidating college students, many of whom have signed up for Partying 101 along with the rest of their studies. The condo could turn into a commune with freeloaders and loud Saturday nights (are you hearing the word "liability?"), and excuses for nonpayment of rent, and a big job while your new student should be studying to get the grades. The resale value of the home after only four years would probably be disappointing—it would have gathered little equity, while interest and closing costs would not have been worked off yet.

You may have raised the most thoughtful, precocious, sensitive, and mature semi-adult on campus. But if you have ever visited campus dorms on weekends during rush or in football season, you will understand that the National Guard is more equipped for this task. This avenue is highly suspect as a well-thought-out tax strategy.

The child care credit

If you pay for eligible child care while working, you may deduct this cost from your taxes. If you pay your babysitter under the table, you will be turning them in to the IRS when you claim the credit care credit. The IRS is suspicious that people are taking in this type of income without paying taxes. So to protect its tax coffers, you must tell them the name and Social Security number of your child care person. They can match this up with their computer and send a nasty letter if the income was not reported. The days are gone for wheeling and dealing in this area.

The maximum you can take is $2,400 for one child or dependent, $4,800 for more than one. This maximum is adjusted based on your income. The lower the income, the greater percentage credit you can take. Check any dependent care company-sponsored assistance plan. This may be more beneficial for those at higher income levels. Some flexible spending plans (part of employee benefit before-tax options) offer child care by an individual or agency in the area, sometimes even on the corporate grounds. More companies are offering this option as working mothers impact the labor market in greater numbers.

The teenage IRA plan

If you have read **Get Rich Slow** or worked through the retirement chapters of this book, you will learn the powerful concept of compound interest in its most awesome form—almost unlimited time. The best way to teach your child about the power of money is to sit down with a scrap of paper and a pencil. Take $2,000 per year, wrap around it an IRA tax shelter, and make six annual payments. After that, let it sit and compound tax free until age 65 (their retirement age will probably be older than that). You can show them they will be a millionaire by that time. Don't tell them, however, that they had *better* be millionaires at that age because of the ravages of inflation over all those years.

Your children have plenty of time to max out their credit cards, to buy a too-expensive home on a 30-year life sentence indentured servant plan, and blow their current income...and more they haven't even made. By planning now for their future, they will have much of the panic out of the way when they get into their fifties, and they will still have the important things they want out of life. If they fund their IRAs now, they can then save the 20% down payment for their home and have enough time to become more successful to really afford a 15- or 20-year mortgage. They can start college funding for their children the day each of your grandchildren are born and live more successfully every year of their lives.

There are additional complicated tax strategies that those with closely-held businesses or other corporations, folks with oodles of money and, therefore, oodles of tax problems, (and people with names like Getty, Gallo, and Rockefeller) can implement. There are trust vehicles (GRITS, GRATS, Crummy trusts, generation skipping trusts, and other very snooty and very expensive methods of tax reduction and passing assets to your children). But if you are one of the yachtless, those outlined here should suffice. Beyond these basics, you should consult attorneys who specialize in these areas.

One caveat: The more control you exert over your assets, the more encumbered they become. Do not paint yourself into a tax corner that may be changed by Congress tomorrow. Consider the lack of control you will give up for tax planning before you go ahead with specific directions. If your attorney thinks trusts are a panacea, get a second opinion. Attorneys get paid when they write documents. Make sure you weigh all sides, including potential conflicts.

Final words of advice: Never have children to make money. Instead, purchase a mink farm or horse breeding ranch. At least you can claim the losses on your tax return!

Chapter 14

Short-Term Money

Short-term money is money you know you need within a three-year time horizon. This could include your emergency fund or "rainy day" money, savings for Christmas, vacation, a new car, real estate taxes, or occasional expenses.

Short-term money can also include any important financial goals which are less than three (3) years away. College might be lurking on the horizon, or retirement may be around the corner. The nature of the goal is not as important as the time frame when the money will be needed. Once we isolate short-term money from long-term money, we will be better able to choose our investment vehicles and allocate our assets in appropriate instruments.

Short-term money should be limited to those investments that offer liquidity as well as marketability. Liquidity means that every dollar put into the investment can be retrieved plus interest. This is a conservative posture which rules out a lot of financial products sold today for short-term investment purposes.

I avoid mortgages and CMOS, ARM funds, bonds and foreign money instruments, and use only money markets that invest exclusively in U.S. Government securities.

This increases the safety of the money, but it also reduces the yield, sometimes significantly. If you must have your money within a short time frame, how could you reproduce it if anything went wrong? So I favor taking the reduction in yield and increasing the safety of principal. For short-term money, I use only lending institutions backed by the FDIC, credit unions, and U.S. Government and agency money market mutual funds. These allow easy access to funds and safety of principal as a first priority.

Money Market Mutual Funds

Taxable money market mutual funds are short-term storage places for emergency assets or rainy day money and as a partial foundation for a long-term investment portfolio.

A money market mutual fund is a large pool of investor money which can only be invested in short-term money securities, such as Treasury bills, corporate IOUs, and other types of short-term debt securities. Time is a risk where money is concerned, and money markets maintain their stability by limiting the maturity of any security which can be bought or sold by the money manager.

All money market mutual funds are not created equal, and the ones I recommend are even duller than most. Money market mutual funds have been the targets of mutual fund company price wars with one upstaging another by offering higher yields. These increased returns often come with increased risk to principal.

Some money markets invest only in U.S. Government Treasury bills. they are considered the safest and return the lowest yields. Others invest in both U.S. Treasury bills and other government agency paper. These are considered reasonably safe because they have some connection with the government who recently has been backing up everyone with public taxpayer money. Still others haven't seen a Treasury bill or government security for fifty miles from the portfolio manager's office. They go for the yield and try to mange the inherent risk as well as possible.

Money market mutual funds are not backed by any specific organization or government agency. They are supported only by the strength of the mutual fund companies who create them and the underlying securities in the asset portfolios. Although there may be few reserves in the FDIC, there is some backing in Washington. Money market funds have no current connection with the Congressional budget.

I view money market mutual funds as risk-free money storage, and I favor snuggling up as close as possible to that risk-free concept. I advocate money markets exclusively investing in U.S. Treasury bills (short-term risk-free government guarantees) or those which invest in a combination of U.S. Treasury bills and government agency issues only. Some government agencies (like Ginnie Maes) are the government itself, while others are an arms-length out from the government. Picky, maybe, but picky may prove prudent.

Most money market mutual funds have a minimum contribution of $1,000 to set up an account, and many have automatic monthly investment plans requiring as little as $25 per month. They come with lots of fringe benefits. You should expect free check writing, free checks, no transaction fees, unlimited checking, and low minimum check amounts (perhaps $100). Additionally, search for telephone redemption and liquidation, and a competitive yield for your category of money market.

How safe is your money market? Don't choose one because is showed up on the top ten list in last month's consumer magazine. Consider only money market funds which do not allow trading in any securities and have no commissions or distribution contingency fees. Frequently financial advisors place investors in money market mutual funds which give the advisor small but continuous commissions. It does not take a rocket scientist to buy and sell Treasury bills. This is wasted money and a tacky—very tacky—move for the financial advisor.

If you are working through a financial advisor, broker, or other investment counselor, check the prospectus to see if you are being charged any of these fees.

If you are tempted to spend money because it is accessible, don't request the check-writing option. Otherwise, always ask for 24-hour access to your funds. This is convenient and important in an emergency, such as an accident or death. I suggest that a third person be put on the signature card in case of a common disaster, especially when parents have young children.

Tax-Exempt Money Markets

Tax-free money market mutual funds are popular for obvious reasons. They are not taxed by the Federal Government. This is not a "free lunch" because tax-free yields are lower. Since they have extra benefits, issues don't have to pay as much to get investors to purchase them.

Investors in high brackets often compare the yields of the tax-free funds with the taxable yields they would have to earn in order to figure out which way to jump (dividing the tax-exempt yield by the formula [1 - the total tax bracket]). On the surface, the decision looks easy. If you're looking at a 4% tax-free yield and can't find better than a 6% yield on a taxable money market, you would think you should invest in a tax-exempt one.

But there is a compelling argument against tax-free money markets. The underlying securities are not backed by the federal government or any of its agencies but, rather, by cities, counties, states, revenue projects, and public institutions like schools and hospitals. The safety of the tax-free bonds changes. Schools, hospitals, and other public projects live on borrowed money, amiable voters, and full state coffers. I see a darkening cloud hovering over municipal bonds for the next two years. Bonds don't just go down in price like IBM. Sometimes they fall off the face of the earth, leaving surprised investors holding thin air. This is no place for anyone's emergency or rainy day fund.

No money market, taxable or tax-free, has defaulted on its shareholders to date. But past performance is no guarantee of future results.

Certificates of Deposit (CDs)

These are individual agreements for time deposits you make with your lender. You are usually paid higher returns when you allow a lending institution to keep your money longer. This allows them to make long-term borrowing decisions and to manage their investment assets better.

Don't deposit all your CDs in one institution, despite FDIC insurance. FDIC reserves can be dangerously low, and if your lender shuts its doors, cash transactions will be disrupted temporarily. The statistical chances of two institutions in the same neighborhood going under at the same time are lower than for one.

CDs are issued with different maturities. Don't be lured into making a long-term deposit unless the interest rate is worth it. You may be sorry in two or three years that you are locked in at lower interest rates when others are receiving much more on their CDs.

The FDIC is an agency of the U.S. Government. It is not "the" U.S. Government. Some day that may become an important distinction. Short-term money should also be diversified into money market mutual funds, just in case.

Collateralized Mortgage Obligations (CMOs)

The Sizzle: A collateralized mortgage obligation (CMO) is a type of mortgage-backed security that offers investors a higher current yield than other alternative fixed income investments. This pass-through type of bond is backed by a pool of conventional fixed rate mortgages as collateral.

Ordinarily as home buyers repay their mortgages, they pay both interest and principal to their lender. It, in turn, passes the money on to mortgage security owners in packaged instruments such as Ginnie Maes, Sallie Maes, Freddie Macs, and Fannie Maes. CMOs, however, attempt to achieve a more predictable cash flow situation with a payment period of interest only. Principal repayment does not begin immediately and cash flows are, therefore, more predictable.

CMOs combine higher yields and quality, and can offer payment of principal and interest on a monthly basis. The monthly basis for interest and principal payments offered with CMOs provides an added opportunity for reinvestment not available from other issues.

The pool of conventional fixed rate mortgages used as collateral for CMOs are typically Ginnie Maes, Freddie Macs and Fannie Maes in a trust. The mortgages underlying these issues carry governmental agency guarantees.

The Steak: As with all investments, CMOs are not without risk. The pace of mortgage-backed securities can fluctuate substantially, especially when interest rates are declining, and more people will refinance their mortgage debt. Changes in the economy and housing markets also affect these issues.

CMOs are not issued or guaranteed by the U.S. Government or its agencies and are subject to market risks. This means that you can't receive higher yields without increased risk. There are numerous varieties of CMOs that are complex to understand, have underlying risks which may not be fully explained by the sales rep, and may not have total liquidity if your funds are needed before being fully paid back.

Investors looking for better alternatives to bank CDs are attracted by CMOs because of the higher yields and the feeling of safety. If redeemed prior to maturity, the value may be less than the original purchase price.

The Bottom Line: PACS, TACS, Companions, Z-bonds, and Sequential Pays are terms you are probably not familiar with. (Please don't *ever* invest in securities you don't understand.) These are all packaged mortgages that brokers have assembled to sell on the street. I don't recommend them, no one understands the risks involved, and I want better control and greater safety of principal from a fixed income vehicle.

One man's poison is another man's opportunity to grab the customer. Faddish, flashy, with underlying securities not backed by the U.S. Government itself (and its trusty printing press), these are not for the faint-hearted—don't risk a lot for a little. Keep your portfolio spread out in the best bank CDs you can rustle up via telephone researching. CMOs are not just CDs with a better interest rate. Higher yields don't always mean smarter banking. Sometimes they mean greater risk of principal.

Sweep Accounts

For a fee, you can receive the latest in interest-bearing checking and money market management—a sweep account.

Such an account offers a range of services all nicely wrapped up in one bundle—checking, investing, borrowing, and short-term storage for funds. Excess (i.e., uninvested) funds are automatically "swept" into short-term interest rate instruments, similar to a money market mutual fund.

It is dubious that a small investor would take advantage of sufficient services to justify the annual fee. However, for a business, a large investor who trades frequently, and for those who want the status, this type of account may be attractive.

Be careful that the opening of your sweep account does not signal a budding relationship with a broker who will introduce you to a different investment world. Until you have significant assets and are capable of losing on individual issues, stick to simple investments for accumulating wealth with serious money. Brokers do not eat well by directing you to bank CDs and no-commission money markets.

Interest-Bearing Checking

So many hybrids have been created by enterprising lenders that it is impossible to categorize them. Some banks offer potential customers a brochure with numerous options for short-term, cost-effective checking.

Just remember that money follows the Golden Rule: The person with the gold makes up the rules. Although consumers carry jingling money in their pockets that is collecting no interest, financial institutions have their interest clocks ticking each second, every minute, all day—even on Sundays. It is important to receive a competitive yield even on short-term emergency fund money. Check a number of lenders, and compare their options with those from other convenient banking institutions.

Weigh the costs of service charges on a "regular" checking account against free-checking combinations of an interest-bearing account with its minimum balance requirements. You should find some optimum combination. Don't hostage any more money in a bank deposit than you must to receive "free" checking, unless its yield is better than that which you could receive in a money market mutual fund.

Chapter 15

Investing for the Long Haul

Fifteen benefits your investment plan should offer

1. **Simplicity.** It should be easy to understand and contain only basic and elementary investment vehicles. No fads, no new and innovative products, and no sophisticated strategies.

2. **Easy management.** This plan should not have to be monitored or altered on a regular basis (no timing). Once the basic asset allocations are set, individual investments should be allowed to work as designed. Only triggering events like enormous market swings, distressed economic conditions or life plan changes should cause the plan to be significantly examined and changed.

3. **Total accessibility.** Every investment should be marketable in a crisis situation, and investment policies should not shrink dollars through surrender charges when the money is recalled.

4. **Window of observation.** The design of the investment should offer the ability to see changes, to follow performance, and to check up on rates of return and security holdings as often as desired.

5. **Cost-effective expenses.** Investment choices should reduce or eliminate costly expenses such as lending institution partners, brokers, and insurance companies. Go directly to the investment vehicle whenever possible.

6. **Flexibility to change investments.** Avoid investments which take many years to develop returns (insurance products) or which charge surrender fees if you want your investment pot early.

7. **Tax advantages whenever prudent.** Do not grab for the tax gimmick before opting for the best investment vehicle. But whenever possible, use tax shelters commonly available. In a 401k or a (403b) Tax Sheltered Annuity, go directly to the investment vehicle instead of an insurance product that charges extra for the insurance wrapping. Your returns will be better if you cut out more intermediaries.

8. **Diversification.** No clairvoyance or forecasting abilities should be employed. Use real common sense diversification to combine investment vehicles that avoid a domino effect and have demonstrated autonomy. Use lots of baskets and different *types* of baskets for your investment nest egg.

9. **Favorable risk-to-return ratio.** Establish an efficient portfolio, maximizing the return, minimizing the risk.

10. **Inflation protection.** Long-term money must constantly seek to outpace the ravages of inflation. So a portion of the portfolio must seek some growth. This means equities (stocks)—and that means careful selection using mutual funds for lower volatility than single stock selection.

11. **No insurance products.** Investment and savings insurance policies and annuities do a mediocre job of both protecting your death protection and providing investment returns. If you want death protection, purchase term insurance outside your investment. Insurance products are costly, succumb to inflation, offer little observation ability, don't accumulate wealth quickly, suffer surrender charges for many years, are usually all managed in-house, and are not instantly accessible.

12. **A portfolio structured for comfort, not for speed.** Lower the risk of loss of principal and diversify over vehicles which have little or no money principal risk but offer lower yields. Let time accumulate compounded returns, and avoid aggressive strategies.

13. **Separate investment accounts.** Investments that are held in the general accounts of institutions such as insurance companies (fixed annuities and most insurance policies) pose risks if the company should become insolvent or shut its doors. You should have a separate investment account which the company cannot tap if it runs into financial trouble. Mutual funds and variable annuities offer this type of protection.

14. **Quality investment vehicles.** Use only the finest investments, those which consistently are praised in consumer magazines. Avoid in-house, clone, or other investments sold by financial companies. All mutual funds are not created equal, and all money markets are not equally sound. Steer clear of name-brand new products that have not weathered the test of time.

15. **Estate planning options.** Qualified or tax-sheltered investments such as IRA accounts, employer compensation, or supplementary voluntary programs such as 401ks or (403b) Tax Deferred Annuities should offer the right for a primary beneficiary and contingent beneficiaries. Taxable and general investment dollars should offer will substitute ownership for ease of estate transfer. If a trust is desired, these should be allowable in a revocable or irrevocable type of trust agreement.

Determining your risk tolerance

How would you react to a loss of $1 out of $10? What about losing $10 out of a $100 investment nestegg? What if $100 of your $1,000 investment principal evaporated overnight? If you woke up tomorrow morning to discover that your $10,000 serious money account had shrunk to $9,000, how cheery would you be for the remainder of the day?

I think I can answer how your stomach would feel if you suddenly were notified that you had suffered a $10,000 loss in your $100,000 retirement account during a stock market or bond market correction. (Investors lived through both disasters in 1987).

Most folks feel they can withstand the loss of small amounts of capital but sicken at even a hint of instant losses of large sums. Each loss in the above examples was only 10%. But as the stakes were raised, the fear of loss had greater negative impact and deeper meaning.

Which dollar is more important to you? The dollar of profit that you might gain through increasing your investment risk? Or the dollar you may lose from increasing your investment capital?

I believe you should concentrate on keeping your principal intact as much as possible, while creating wealth and beating inflation on a slow but steady pace. People take needless investment risks because they do not understand the risk versus return rules and they cannot correctly assess investment risks in this fluctuating and uncertain (sometimes even psychotic) economic environment.

It is reasonable to expect a 10% to 12% total return on a portfolio mix of bank Certificates of Deposit, money market mutual funds (with U.S. Treasury and U.S. Agencies as underlying investments), and conservative equity income mutual funds as a final ingredient. To instead invest a majority of capital into stocks or stock mutual funds may increase an investor's profit potential by 50% while heightening the risk of loss to principal by *200%* or more.

The risk accelerates *more* and the return potential expands *less* for each percentage point above a certain diversification of investments. In other words, going for twice the profits may equal four or five times the risk of losing serious investment money.

Playing the markets

When a company needs money, it can do one of two things: (1) Ask for a loan or issue bonds; or (2) invite others to own a piece of (equity) the company—issue stock. The corporation searches for an underwriter (usually a large brokerage house or investment banking firm), who decides things like the initial price of the securities and how they will be marketed. After promising to sell the entire issue (a firm commitment), the underwriter gives the company a pile of money, with which it trots off to produce more widgets.

The underwriter then offers these securities for public sale. Once these new securities are in the hands of investors, a secondary market sprouts where investors can buy and sell their securities to others at prices agreed on by both the buyer and the seller. This auction is a simple description of the stock and bond markets.

Imagine you have just inherited $10,000 and are excited about becoming your own money manager. You finally have a meaty amount of investment capital to work with. Now you could spend weeks, months, perhaps even years pouring over charts and researching markets, margins, and muni ratings. Or you could choose a company you already recognize as stable and profitable, such as IBM. Though you can't buy a great many shares of IBM at nearly $100 a share, you are confident that your investment is relatively "safe" (there is that deceptive word again) and will earn lucrative profits through both dividends and stock growth in the future.

Your stock shares confidently advance for a while, but then turn sluggish, due to the economy and a saturation of the market. When another company introduces a competitive computer at a lower cost to the consumer, your stock becomes depressed (like you) and begins to deteriorate.

At first you are not concerned. But the stock doesn't reverse and continues its slide down, down, down. You become very concerned, perhaps even panicked. Should you sell out at a loss or hang in until it goes up again? Finally, in desperation, you liquidate (near the bottom), suffer a financial and emotional loss, and vow that your investing days are over. You place what's left of your investment capital into a bank CD.

You have lived through the classic mistake of novice investing: You put all your eggs into one basket. You originally picked IBM because you were familiar with the company's reputation. However, you were *not* familiar with the dynamics that a company like IBM must compete in, the risks of high-tech competition, the accelerated product obsolescence, the intense competition for market share, the time frames for this size of corporation to adapt, or even how these markets track. You lost investment capital. You also missed the chance (your opportunity cost) to own other investments that could have made profits.

Finally, inflation continued to move up while your stock slid in the opposite direction. For a final blow, you gave up on investing to outpace inflation and incorrectly placed all your assets into a "safer" fixed-income vehicle, one guaranteed to lag behind inflation, year after year.

Take your ball and go home

Individual stocks, even those of mature companies, should be ignored until an investor has amassed at least $150,000 (excluding all real estate) in a combination of bank Certificates of Deposit, money market mutual funds, and conservative, well-diversified mutual funds. Only then should a novice consider throwing darts at single issues to fund serious investment goals.

A small number of quality stocks in a large portfolio can be helpful on a long-term basis. They can shelter growth without current tax consequences until they are sold—only annual dividends are taxed. Stocks can show spontaneous spurts of growth faster than diversified mutual funds.

Monolithic mature companies offer a lower return than equity income or growth mutual funds, perhaps with no greater safety of principal. So avoid older mature companies. You must worry more about conservation of purchasing power over long periods of time than protection of principal. Stocks should be added with the sole purpose of increasing investment returns, not lowering the overall performance of the portfolio.

Stay away from new corporations with innovative products, services or methodology that is faddish. These have too much price volatility, tremendous growing pains, follow wide market swings and enjoy honeymoon periods.

Even for those who can afford it, I recommend a small proportion (10%) of a total portfolio invested in individual stock issues. It is difficult to find stocks that rival mutual fund performance on a consistent basis. Why take extra risks on capital, when you may receive even better overall returns and certainly greater diversification through mutual funds?

Plan on holding stock selections for many years. When they have accumulated serious dollars, consider partially selling off (even with the tax consequences) and reducing systematic risk. Defer those profits into a variety of other vehicles.

When inheriting a stock portfolio or contemplating what to do with an ESOP stock plan, consider selling off a certain percentage of the stock on an annual basis to reduce your overall position and exposure to a single issue.

Creating an effective mutual fund portfolio will rival any millionaire's investment ledgers, offer less risk than individual stocks or bonds, and may provide higher returns.

Over-the-counter stocks

The Sizzle: You may get in on the ground floor of the next IBM or Xerox. Small companies have experienced tremendous growth in recent years, and the potential for fast profits and escalated returns are more possible with these smaller companies that the market has generally not yet recognized.

Everyone knows names of companies that gained fame overnight with a new product, a medical cure or approved drug, or a high-tech innovation. The lure of windswept returns and relatively small prices per share of stock makes these attractive to the smaller investor with few assets.

The Steak: Small companies are, in general, thinly traded, suffer wide swings in price, are particularly vulnerable to the risks of most markets, may be undercapitalized and suffer greatly from one product liability suit or prolonged delays in product approval. This market can be a sucker's bet. Brokers solicit small companies via phone, and attract investors by selling greed. Smaller companies don't just move down in price like the Fortune 500 giants. Sometimes they literally fall off the face of the earth, victims of early mortality.

The Bottom Line: Avoid this market for potential fast returns. This is no place for serious money and small investors. These markets are fast, can be easily manipulated without your knowledge, and have a reputation for being overpriced (the broker's or market maker's profit) and offering little purchasing and selling competition from the few bidders interested in these smaller issues.

For gambling purposes, stick to the thoroughbreds and the $2 betting window or the one-armed Vegas bandits where you *know* your odds are poor and your losses will be small.

New issues

The Sizzle: Here's yet-another groundfloor opportunity. Prices are affordable on new issues, and though riskier because they have no track record, the potential for growth should also be enhanced.

You will most likely be introduced to IPOs—initial public offerings (new stock companies or new stock issues of existing corporations)—from a call by a stockbroker. Your regular broker also has deals that come through the company, issues the broker/dealer may have underwritten. The lure of large profits from a small ante sells new stock or bond issues.

The Steak: If this deal is so great, why is your broker telling *you* about it instead of buying every share legally allowed for him- or herself? If the brokerage has underwritten the stock or bond issue, they probably own it and must peddle it to make money. If it is a hot issue (so good that it is snapped up as soon as it goes public), it is doubtful you will ever hear about it unless you are a large client.

Initial public offerings have an underwriting fee that causes a markup in the price beyond what the underwriting syndicate feels it will sell on the open bidding market. If you want to investigate these for real money, don't buy them until *after* they hit the public auction market. At that time they will be trading without the dealer markup and will probably, therefore, be cheaper.

The Bottom Line: If your broker was really interested in you, he or she would not be calling to get you to buy the higher priced shares with the deal markup but would, instead, let you know that something good will hit the market soon and you may be able to pick up a great bargain (without a broker/dealer underwriting fee) once it starts to publicly trade. Avoid these except for curiosity sake. Too much risk, not enough return, and too much middleman.

A penny for your...company?

The Sizzle: "Penny stocks" are usually priced at less than $5 per share, and many seem attractive because the necessary investment capital is minimal and the potential for lucrative profits seems enormous. If a dollar stock moves up just *one more dollar,* to only $2.00 per share, you will make a *100%* return on your investment. There are several national penny stock newsletters that discuss and even advise novice investors as to which markets, which industries, and which individual companies are ideal candidates for speculative consideration. The lure of quick profits with little money down appeals to many investors who otherwise could not afford to purchase equities.

Purchasing 100 shares of a pollution control corporation for $50 plus commissions may seem downright cheap and a one-time, not-to-be-missed opportunity.

The Steak: This style of investing is akin to gambling. Aside from the round-trip commissions (the cost for buying and subsequently selling the stocks) which the investor must recover, the current price of a stock may be locked in at its low price...because that is exactly what it is worth. The market is telling those who can translate the message that the stock is not worth even 1¢ more than its current price.

Speculation is no way to create long-term assets for serious financial goals. If you need some excitement in your weekends and don't want to walk 18 holes for enjoyment, take your green fee money and try your hand at these markets. But never let a broker talk you into sending large sums of capital into these high-risk high-fliers.

Cold-call cowboys sell these types of stock issues via telephone solicitations. Their company may have underwritten the stock and now has an inventory sitting on their shelves. The broker's job is to create a mark-up (make their profit) by transferring ownership from them to you. They lure you with promises and use greed as their tool. Making it big, with only a few dollars and no hard work, is their theme, and with their expertise and knowledge in this area, how can you go wrong? After all, there is risk involved in crossing the street.

The Bottom Line: The only risk they have is the likelihood that you will hang up on them before they can motivate you to write a check. Once you have complied, you are the only one risking anything. Never purchase anything over the phone, and stay away from cheap high-risk deals. You may believe you can pick the next Xerox, IBM, or Apple Computer, but chances are you will be buying Fred's Guitars, Tyrone's Toxic Waste Control, or Monty's Medical Cures, all of which will crash and burn soon after your purchase.

Options

The Sizzle: Crisis or opportunity—you can benefit financially from both. The epitome of leveraged investing, options allow the investor to predict a particular market direction, to think highly enough of one's opinions to bet investment capital on future activity in that specific market, and to subsequently collect a much higher profit for the extra risk during the investment period.

The old standards—stocks, bonds and mutual funds—may form a basic foundation for your investment portfolio, but if you don't have an investment advisor who is showing you these types of opportunities, you are not maximizing your profit potential. To survive and prosper in the future, the aggressive investor should confront new and innovative frontiers. The commodities markets offer such opportunities due to quickly changing prices in areas such as coffee, sugar, heating oil, metals, lumber, stocks and even domestic or foreign currencies. With each economic disaster there exists a silver lining—an opportunity to profit financially—if you are quick to spot that window of opportunity.

For the more qualified investor, these markets offer the opportunity to out-perform more traditional investments and take control of large quantities of certain commodities for relatively small option premiums.

The Steak: This is not an investment for wimps. You must be willing to lose big without crying over spilled dollars and without betting next week's grocery budget on your guesstimate. This is speculation, not investing.

The options and futures markets move quickly, and brokers urge you to act immediately. They call this your "window of opportunity." Actually, the longer you sit on your checkbook, the smaller *their* window of opportunity. If you think about their offer long enough, you may come to your senses and put your checkbook away. If you let these vendors pressure you into acting, you will plunk down your money and take your chances, which are not good at all.

Trading options makes an aggressive growth mutual fund look like a walk in the park. If you wince at stock market crashes, you should avoid these types of investment losses. Limited loss, in this connotation, means losing up to 100% of your investment capital. The high degree of leverage obtainable in options trading can result in quick losses even in a temporarily declining or escalating market. Like a fulcrum balancing a moving teeter-totter, due to the large amount of a commodity under your control, small price changes can affect your proportionately smaller amount of risk capital.

The bold point disclosures and warnings wouldn't be etched in dark lettering, capital letters (or both) if someone else (a regulatory body) didn't demand them. And the regulators wouldn't force companies to make such disclosures if naive but greedy investors had not previously lost lots of money in this speculation game.

It would take you years to understand, let alone predict, these types of markets. In-the-money, out-of-the-money, puts, and calls are not terms you cut your teeth on. If you are reading this book as your guide to investment prowess, you are definitely not a candidate for options of any kind.

Futures

The Sizzle: I can't bear to set you up with a salivating salespitch, but I will tell you if you like the sound of limited risk profits, you will love the potential returns you can dream about from *un*limited risk—risking not just your investment capital but a stake in your new home, your IRA accounts, your spouse, the kids, and the family pooch to boot.

The commodity futures firms won't actually threaten to take your family away (creditors never want college preparatory teenagers and pets). They may, however, suggest that in order to stay out of jail and repay the money owed to them when your market went south, you may want to sell them for whatever you can negotiate. Are you beginning to understand what unlimited risk *really* means?

The Steak: In the options section above, the most you could lose was 100% of your investment capital plus commission and trading fees (gee, thanks). If you call that limited risk, I have a bridge that I would like to show you. Now for the benefits of unlimited risk.

Investments in commodities futures have an even higher lever of risk associated with them because you are actually contracting a legal agreement regarding future prices of items such as platinum, gold, coffee, sugar, and oil without a crystal ball. This agreement is not backed up by a small option to purchase or to sell but by an actual *agreement to take possession* of a particular commodity or to sell it at a later date at a price you name now. This agreement will stand no matter how much you may have to pay to purchase or how low you may have to sell the commodity in the future. Fools may walk where angels fear to tread, but even a fool shouldn't be strolling through these markets. These should be limited to filthy rich folks who won't notice a $50,000 or $100,000 drop in their investment portfolio.

As commodity prices fluctuate (spike or tank) on a daily basis, the market value of a customer's investment account also increases or decreases. Resulting gains or losses are recorded, and buyers and sellers of futures contracts may be required to maintain sufficient deposit funds to cover losses that might be incurred as a result of adverse price changes.

If your market moves against you (does the opposite of what you bet hard-earned money on), you will be called on to deposit additional funds on short notice or to fund additional capital to maintain your current market position. Even if your position is liquidated at a loss, you will be liable for any resulting deficit in your account.

Under certain volatile market conditions, it may be difficult or even impossible to trade (liquidate) your position. This may result in even larger investment losses than anticipated. The suitability of this speculative arena should be limited to those who regularly bet on such longshots as the Christians over of the lions. The odds, in my opinion, are about equal.

I'm Uncle Sam, I am, I am

The Sizzle: Investors are increasingly looking to Treasury securities for safety of principal and a competitive return. Many are turning to Treasury bills, short-term investments of 6 -, 9 -, or 12-month terms.

These are backed by the full faith and taxing power of the U.S. Government. Interest earned is not subject to taxation until maturity. Treasury bills (T-bills) are also exempt from many state and local income taxes.

T-bills do not quote a stated interest rate. Instead they are auctioned off and the buyer's earnings are calculated through the difference between the purchase price and the face value of the bill at maturity. This difference is called the discount. Minimum investments start at $10,000.

The Steak: Safety of principal should only represent part of your investment criteria. Though many retirees choose T-bills as their weapon of choice, they are further reducing their net worth because of inflationary pressures. Safety of principal is commendable, but not at the price of erosion of dollars from inflation. There is a guaranteed loss of dollars over time when a significant amount of funding is directed toward low-paying investments such as T-bills.

The Bottom Line: At $10,000 a throw, you can't diversify the average portfolio too well. For long-term money, avoid T-bills in large amounts and the instinct to flee toward safety. No one will give you any more for your dollars than they have to, not even you own government.

United States Savings Bonds

The Sizzle: Bonds issued by the United States Government are considered risk free from default. In fact, the only bond that you can purchase that does not suffer from some risk of default (the bond becomes worthless) is one which is issued by your own insolvent government. Though the government is the largest debtor (in even deeper doo-doo than the consuming public), it has the full power to tax you and everybody else and pledges its full (considerable) assets behind every bond.

Savings (Series EE) bonds purchased by parents for a child's college education can be tax-free at redemption time. They are convenient to purchase through payroll deductions, easy to store, and understandable. A bond purchased for $25 today will mature in approximately 12 years for the value of $50. That is 100% return on your investment with absolutely no risk of your principle.

Taxes can be deferred until you sell the bond, or they can be paid on an annual basis. Ownership of savings bonds can be accomplished in a variety of ways, either in an individuals's name, co-ownership, or even in a child's name. The strongest investment paper you can buy is issued by the U.S.

Government's promise of timely interest and return of principal at maturity.

The Steak: A $25 bond purchased today with a face value of $50 will be worth $25 when you cash it in at maturity. Savings bonds are one of the worst fixed-income vehicles with regard to inflation.

You will never be able to fund any large financial objective—such as college tuition or retirement planning—primarily through the use of U.S. Government Savings Bonds unless you direct a lot more of your investments than you want toward any specific long-term goal. No one wants to give you any more for your money to get you to hand it over than they have to. and that includes your own government.

The Bottom Line: Great gifts for Christmas or birthdays instead of the clothes (which later find a home at the back of a closet) or the toys (that are broken within thirty minutes of opening). But a 6% return, not even a *tax-exempt* 6%, can't run fast enough to match the 8% to 10% inflation of today's educational institutions. This is long-term money and must be put on a faster track.

Wrap accounts

With the overwhelming popularity of mutual funds for the small investor to gain equal footing into investment arenas previously reserved for institutional clients, it was only natural that brokerages, money management firms, and insurance companies would want to share in lucrative management fees that mutual funds have garnered over the last ten years. Today you can hire your own private money manager or "superstar" to look after your smaller bundle of investment assets.

The Sizzle: This product has tremendous appeal for the middle class and those seeking increased status to separate themselves from the masses. What great cocktail conversation to casually drop some investment tidbits discussed during a telephone conversation or personal visit with your individually hired portfolio manager.

In addition to the snob appeal these new services represent, hiring a money expert and choosing either a conservative or aggressive money management philosophy means consolidation and progress to investors with portfolios too large to actively manage themselves, too small to interest a nationally recognized money mogul (expert). Instead of throwing darts at the Wall Street stock pages and spending time better allotted to their own business pursuits, professionals and upwardly mobile middle-income folks can hire someone to understand investment markets and utilize their expertise to achieve better overall returns.

Personal money managers can be bought to look after as little as $50,000 in the wrap-fee market. You can usually interview and choose your own money expert from a list most brokerages and boutique companies provide. These managers are "on the same page" with your investment preferences. You pay an annual charge of from 1.5% to 3%—higher fees should reflect either greater exposure to equities (stocks), more client services, a better quality or more famous money manager, or all of the above. This includes all expenses of purchasing and selling securities, management fees, monitoring your portfolio's performance and progress, and sending you updated quarterly account statements.

A client completes a questionnaire to establish risk tolerances, a basic profile, investment objectives, and time horizons. He or she may interview several money managers before deciding which expert will run their portfolio.

The Steak: Your broker or insurance company wants to manage your money. Now that it's more difficult to peddle stocks and other products, companies are selling their services as money managers. Instead of feast or famine, these corporations can provide themselves with a consistent cash flow (an annuity) by locking in investment capital to manage on an ongoing basis. The fees are steep compared with the annual expense ratios and management fees for most mutual funds with proven track records. Another advantage of mutual funds is that "tracking them" merely requires purchasing any major newspaper.

These accounts have great sex appeal for the status conscious, and they offer extra conveniences. But at what cost to your total return? You pay an annual fee, are unable to keep continuous track of your investments, unable to watch over the experts' shoulders, and may do no better than you could have done yourself. With you at the helm and with systematic risk reduced through high quality diversification, you may even lose less principal when markets turn sour. You will invest your money more carefully because your future depends on your choices. You will understand how serious any investment decisions are.

Discretionary accounts, those in which a money manger makes all investment decisions without your regular input, can be dangerous. If any triggering event makes it necessary to review or consider changing any of my clients' asset mixes, I firmly believe we should sit down and have a heart-to-heart talk. I want my clients in charge of their money, not a money manager miles away. I want my clients involved in all asset allocation decisions, and their approval for all investment directions that I may recommend. More money has been lost by naive clients who trusted someone else and put a stranger in charge of their money. Asset allocation does not have to be complicated to work effectively.

There is no status in overpaying. Mutual funds will costs you less and give you 24-hour access to performance statistics and your account values through your local newspaper and your telephone. The funds offer the flexibility to liquidate immediately, or to change your investment strategies at a month's notice.

Don't give up your role as money manager and decision-maker. Check out the track records of all-weather mutual funds in both good and poor market environments, and keep your eye on those you choose. With similar track records compared with privately managed money, lower annual fees, and your ability to control your investment at all times, wrap accounts get two thumbs down from me. I want someone to fuss over me for my intrinsic value and because they really care about me, not for my investment account.

12. The bottom line

If you had $500,00 or $1,000,000 laying around, it would be feasible, perhaps even beneficial, to purchase a private money manager or take on the full-time responsibility of choosing individual stocks, bonds, and cash instruments (CDs and Treasury bills). With this much money,. you would have sufficient capital to spread around for diversification (to avoid systematic risk). But with $5,000, $10,000 or as little as $25 per month, heavy investment diversification is not possible. At least not if you pick the companies by yourself.

By heavily diversifying your investment capital, you will likely limit your upside potential for higher appreciation and greater profits. You will not have much chance for spectacular returns. But you will also avoid the spectacular losses and downturns, the plummeting roller coaster rides through economic and business cycles, market changes, and interest rate collapses and relapses. If you take out the peaks and valleys of investing, you will have a more comfortable ride with only small bumps in the highway pavement that you can live with.

Chapter 16

How to (Not)
Play the Market

"Do not gamble,
take all of your savings and buy some stock
and hold on to it till it goes up,
then sell it.
If it don't go up,
don't buy it."
—Will Rogers

Unless you have the dollars to burn (or lose), remember that I do not generally recommend your buying individual stocks and bonds. That's what mutual funds are for. Presuming you don't want to listen—or that you are merely curious about what everyone else who isn't listening to me is doing—let's look at some of the ways, strange and otherwise, that amateurs and professionals supposedly "predict" what the market's going to do.

Mary, Mary, quite contrary

The *contrarian* marches to a different drummer. If everyone is buying bonds, the contrarian is selling them. If there is a rush toward "small cap" industrial stocks or basic value issues (this is important "investment-ese" jargon to learn for cocktail parties), the contrarian is scurrying in the opposite direction. Contrarians are bottom-fishermen, buying throwaways or overlooked opportunities in the marketplace.

There is actually some sense in this. Historically, the next market swing comes soon after the majority of experts decide the opposite. When 60% of the money gurus are satisfied that the bull market is in full swing, it seems prudent to consider that the bear may already be at the door.

Everyone's goal is to "beat the market." But how can you beat the market if you *are* the market, if you're just doing what everybody else is? When everyone is buying, prices increase. When significant profit-taking (selling) takes place, prices decline. Similar to buyer and seller real estate markets, prices depend on how much competition exists and how "hot" the property seems. Like all auctions, excited buyers bid up prices.

Contrarians have a large responsibility but limited avenues. They must balance the opposite side of every teeter-totter. They must counter major trends by acting in an opposite fashion. They must also be emotionally secure, because everyone is always pointing fingers at them, insisting they are out of step.

The PMS Market Theory

What do October 19, 1987, October 13, 1989, and October, 1991 have in common? The first two were stock market nightmares. The last was expected to be a repeat performance.

This particular PMS (Past Market Strategy) prediction relied on two investing fundamentals: (1) bad things come in threes, and (2) the Dow Jones plunges were both suffered in October in each of the past two odd-numbered years. There was more than casual observation of these correlations among even the credible market watchers as October, 1991 approached. Others argued against this prediction by noting that the frenetic buying during the merger mania epic was absent and hot air stock prices did not surface this time around. Point and counterpoint. But no one openly scoffed at this method of market analysis, and only the hushed, hollow laughter of superstition-bashers could be heard.

Note that this is but one of a myriad of possible theories that attempt to predict what tomorrow will be based on what yesterday was. Here's another one.

Pigskin predicting

If you favor Monday Night Football over pouring through the money section of the *Wall Street Journal,* you can still win the investing game. Your talent may be picking pigskin winners, and that means you have a 9 out of 10 chance to predict next year's stock market. Here's how:

Over 90% of the time in the last 21 years, when the National Football Conference emerged as the Super Bowl victor, the following year saw general gains for the stock market. And vice versa—when the American Football Conference won, the market would decline.

So, according to this theory at least, gamble your investment money based on your football gambling.

For those of you who don't get it—*Just because this correlation exists means absolutely nothing about what the market will actually do next year.*

The Lemming Law

Lemmings are furry, mole-like animals with short tails. They are the ultimate "groupies," and, when over-populated, rush headlong to the sea and drown themselves.

The lemmings mirror a group of faceless investors who follow the fads. In other words, if my neighbor has one, I should really consider buying two. This is similar to buying on the advice of others, but lemmings don't buy for safety or out of fear—they deeply believe they are astute investment minds with a winning edge over the pack.

Their investment lives depend on classics like direct mail newsletters they glean for between-the-line clues of what to purchase next. Instead of realizing that "hot" inside information will have cooled considerably by the time they hear about it, they leap into action, convinced they have discovered a market aspect everyone else has overlooked.

Lemmings think they take part in shrewd investment and tax maneuvers, and are not shy about reporting their supposed successes to others. If they purchase an investment for

$25,000, then sell it 20 years later for $50,000, they advertise their astounding 100% return on investment capital. Never mind that over the 20-year period, that return translates into a very unastounding annual rate of 3.5 %...not counting buying and selling costs.

They reject new information and common-sense logic because they believe they already *have* all the important criteria locked away in their heads. You can't teach lemmings anything new. They already know it all.

The saddest and most serious aspect of lemmings is that they never realize their basic investment mistakes and continue with the same ones throughout their lives. They never effectively work their money.

Every lemming has a scheme for getting rich that will not work. Lemmings have taught me that nature, indeed, sides with the hidden flaw.

Group grope advocates

This is the category into which most investors fall. They have been taught that managing money is complicated and intimidating and certainly should not e attempted by those who merely make it. The financial industry preaches this philosophy as if it had been handed down as the Eleventh Commandment.

There are financial supermarkets which claim they are so large, they do it all. There are small boutiques whose sales reps show you rooms full of computer technology that will be watching your money 24 hours per day (even while you sleep), timing your investment moves. What investment will you be in that could possibly demand that kind of stealth bomber defense system? If the night janitor accidentally pulls the plug while cleaning, is there a backup plan for momentary attack? These claims are ludicrous and impossible promises which will just cost you needless advisory fees and expense.

Brand-name institutions, like supermarket products, generally cost more. The "bigger is better" mentality says absolutely nothing about the quality of solutions for your financial challenges. Their job is to get you to their cash register, not over your financial finish line.

Buy information, not financial products. Then synthesize the material yourself, and make your own decisions.

Group-grope investors are frightened instead of cautious. They move with everyone else and are comforted by claims of security and safety. They can be seduced with promises of greed because they know little about the financial world around them.

Group gropers listen to everyone who solicits them and become confused because every "expert" has a different direction. They are attracted to bells and whistles (like tax-deferred and tax-free products) and never realize what they are investing in. They listen to sales pitches as intently as if those promises were true. Group gropes usually buy the sizzle, seldom get to eat the steak.

Tulipmania

When tulips were introduced into seventeenth century Holland, an agricultural land of modest economic pursuits, they became a fad of monstrous proportions. Before long nearly every citizen had given up normal landscaping for a small plot of tulip bulbs. The aristocracy saw spectacular investment opportunities. Soon tulip fields filled most of Holland's land surface.

Tulipmania grew so fast that soon there were tulip laws, tulip contracts, and tulip options (puts and calls) on tulip contracts. Confident investors executed purchases without blooming guarantees or even the slightest intent of taking actual delivery of the bulbs by quickly re-selling their contracts to higher bidders.

Tulip notaries stamped out legal protection tulip quality guarantee documents, and special tulip centers were established exclusively for tulip trading and speculating. There seemed no upper limit to the price one might pay for a unique breeder bulb. At one point, option contracts called "windhandel" (prophetically translated into trading air) were as common as today's corn, soybean, coffee, or pork belly (pig) futures markets.

Even tulip bubbles burst, and the excesses of the period turned into a soberingly spectacular fall. Tulip prices went down in flames, There were no Jacks with their infinitely growing beanstalks, and lawsuits filled the courts at such rates that the dockets were backed up for years.

As you read this historical synopsis, insert any American group think you identify with (or have invested in): our national debt, the gold rush of the 1970s, the stock market crash of 1929 and again in 1986, the bull market of the 1980s, real estate runups (residential and commercial development), merger megalomania, and/or the junk bond era, to name a few.

With any speculative mania, once a trend is established, emotion becomes instrumental in accelerating momentum and bidding up prices—gold went public at $35 per ounce but peaked at over $800 per ounce. Credible experts in the field add their approvals, and confusion of purpose clouds rational analysis. Overgenerous investment capital is diverted to the specific sector, further escalating initial investor profits quickly. The fast gains fuel further speculation and more dollars invested.

Up to a certain point, capital infusion produces good profit results. But when the general public enters *en masse,* hubris (euphoria or infallibility) sets in. Reckless investing with little research by those acting out of greed and fear set the final stage. The Greater Fool theory reigns as investors overbuy, content that, though they overpaid, a greater fool will pay them even more. This pushes prices higher. At the peak, those who can least afford to lose, to wait patiently for profits, and who are not knowledgeable are firmly entrenched and heavily involved.

A mistake in timing, a rumor picked up by the media, or other glitch unravels the upward spiral in a hurry, and the original process reverses. The fall takes on a panic atmosphere, and prices plummet. As the trumpets of doom sound, overreaction causes prices to overcorrect.

Then the smoke clears, the pieces are swept away, and the public's painful lesson is etched into memory—until the next enticing opportunity knocks. Short public memories are symbols that we learn little from historical mistakes and are anxious to repeat our own.

Carpe Diem (Seize the day)

Based on all the foregoing, it may now seem pretty obvious that novices should individually avoid the stock market. But based on such strategies, so should most professionals, at least with *your* money. The similarity between you throwing darts at the stock page to construct your portfolio and hiring a professional to do that for you is that *both* of you will lose *your* money. In addition, you will pay fees and expenses to a money guru.

According to performance charts, the pros haven't done much better than know-nothing small investors and dartboard portfolios like the *Forbes* Dartboard Fund.

Whether you research the new Frequent Near Miss Airline mutual fund you read about last week or trust your broker's advice regarding the Monkey Mart initial public offering he couldn't wait to show you, no one has a 50-yardline seat to look into the future. So let's stop pretending we can organize unrelated and coincidental facts into infallible investment strategies and investment returns or accurately predict the stock, bond or other markets any more than we can guess under which bridge the turnpike police will hide.

Start using common sense fundamentals to accumulate wealth, comfortably and surely.

Chapter 17

Mutual Fund-amentals

What is a mutual fund? Simply put, it is a large pool of investor dollars, managed by an individual or a team of portfolio managers, and actively directed toward a specific investment goal spelled out in the mutual fund prospectus.

Mutual funds range in size from a few million dollars in total assets to large monoliths that rival the gross national product of some foreign nations. Some funds are managed by a lone professional, while others are directed by several people, a committee approach.

What are the advantages of mutual funds over purchasing individual stocks, bonds, or other investment vehicles? If you have a $1 million dollar portfolio, maybe little. But if you are working with much less, mutual funds can give you the diversification of a millionaire's portfolio to reduce risk. Mutual funds offer:

1. The potential for higher investment returns than through intermediaries such as lending institutions and insurance companies.
2. Greater control over investment capital.
3. An inflation hedge against long-term purchasing power erosion.
4. Greater insight into where the money is invested.
5. Greater returns when the mutual fund does better.
6. The flexibility to change investment goals easily.
7. Redemption and withdrawal flexibility.

8. Instant liquidity through money market mutual funds with check-writing privileges.
9. Diversification to soften investment risk.
10. Numerous types to satisfy every investment palate.
11. Tax-free investing options.
12. Tax shelters such as IRAs, 401ks, TSAs, SEPs, KEOGHs, and UGMAs.
13. Estate planning objectives (e.g. avoiding probate).
14. Separate accounts away from the general fund of the parent company.
15. Investment programs for as little as $25 a month.
16. Automatic withdrawal programs for regular monthly income.
17. Professional money management previously available to the affluent.
18. Relatively small management fees and overhead expenses.
19. Economics of scale, such as volume discounts.
20. Automatic reinvestment of dividends, interest, and capital gains for future growth.
21. Telephone exchanges and redemptions.
22. Numerous options for price discounts.
23. 24-hour, up-to-date, telephone-access information regarding your investment funds and accounts.
24. Simplified record-keeping.
25. Daily access to your investment through media news reporting.

What do you invest in when you buy a mutual fund? If you can think of a possibility, there are probably a number of funds that include it in their portfolios...and at least one that *specializes* in it. There are stock, bond, money market, biotech, health care, gold, health science, natural resource, tax-free, environmental, Ginnie Mae, socially responsible (good money), junk bond, U.S. Government, and mortgage-packed mutual funds, to just skim the surface.

There are so many mutual funds that a small investor could spend months studying them and still be confused. Good quality mutual funds can be purchased for a minimum lump sum of $1,000 or as little as $25 per month. It has been said there is a mutual fund for every investor.

Mutual funds cut out the financial middleman. Lending institutions and insurance companies are private profit-making corporations, while mutual funds are taxed as investor pass-throughs. They are only allowed to keep disclosed fees and expenses. All other profits must be passed on to the shareholders (investors).

Investors pool their money, and the fund management selects the various securities. Therefore, each investor owns a small piece of the whole pie, not just certain companies or securities. Most mutual funds offer statements of investment so you can research how diversified your investment money will be. All mutual funds provide a prospectus, the basic investment contract that investors should be able to understand thoroughly.

Get it in writing

The mutual fund prospectus (written investment company contract) sets forth the basic investment policies that will be utilized by management. That investment philosophy cannot be significantly changed except by a majority vote of all shareholders (owners of the fund).

If a mutual fund prospectus states that it will invest in U.S. company stocks with records of high-paying dividends, it will not pick up attractively priced bio-tech companies. If a mutual fund claims it will invest only in U.S. stocks and bonds, you will never own a part of a Philippine railroad. The prospectus is the most valuable tool you can use to choose which mutual fund will fit into your future investment plans.

Investment-ease

Many mutual funds allow automatic monthly investment plans through payroll deductions or your checking account.

This is ideal for paying yourself first and setting up and meeting consistent long-term investment objectives. Small contributions on a monthly basis over a period of years may be the difference between saving the money you need for college or retirement or falling short.

If your investment objectives change, your money can be transferred via phone to other more appropriate funds in (or out of) the same mutual fund family.

Mutual funds are ideal investment vehicles for tax-sheltered accounts such as IRAs, 401ks, 403bs, TDAs, TSAs, and any other employee pension plans. They can be used by the self-employed for SEPs, KEOGHs, for children's accounts (UGMAs), and more.

Now you see it, now you don't

Mutual funds were created with the Investment Act of 1940, and each fund is a separate investment company with its own portfolio manager and unique investment policy and objectives. Mutual funds are separated from the mutual fund parent company accounts by law to insure that the health of a mutual fund rests solely on the securities in the investment pool.

The separate investment account is a critical feature and may become more important in the future as more financial corporations struggle through some tough times. Your college or retirement fund must be accessible when you need it, not when the investment company becomes healthy and decides to re-open its doors for business as usual. Your investment performance should depend on the value of the assets in your portfolio, not on how well the parent company manages its own business affairs.

Easy does it

Mutual funds tend to change more slowly and appear less volatile than individual securities because they are comprised of many individual components that may act completely differently. Therefore, changes in the financial barometers, interest rate surprises, and market swings may affect the well-diversified types less. They can be considerably less volatile (risky) than owning individual stocks and bonds.

Since mutual funds are tracked daily in major newspapers, you can always know exactly how much money you have in your fund account. Simply multiply the total shares you own by the sell price you find beside your mutual fund. Investors can follow their investments on a daily basis if they choose. This is perhaps the strongest argument for investing in mutual funds: current information, control of the investment funds, and accessibility to your money.

How big is too big?

I prefer those funds with significant total assets—between $500 million and $2 billion dollars—yet not as large as some emerging growth countries. Smaller funds may not attract top management without the ability to pay higher salaries and incentives. Larger funds can purchase volume securities without unbalancing other assets in the portfolio. They can negotiate better prices and have more cash available to meet investor redemptions.

Funds can get *too* large. Enormous mutual funds can suffer from taking on too much freight, like a large ship on a small lake. Financial markets are choppy seas, and even a genius cannot turn around a freighter easily. Fine-tuning a huge fund is impossible. I myself prefer a mid-sized leaner vessel that can respond quickly, remove ballast (poor securities) without sinking further, and be ready for frequent surprises. Some huge mutual funds have lagged significantly in recent years.

Meet the boss

The portfolio manager of a mutual fund makes the basic buy and sell decisions. Not all managers are equally talented, and it will take some research to select those who have consistently managed well.

This does not, however, mean that you should choose those managers with the highest returns over the last 10 years. Some managers achieve higher yields by taking even greater risks with investor capital. You must do some investigation into the manager's rating (their *alpha)* as compared with others in the same asset class.

Gender is no measure of a qualified portfolio manager. Some of the best funds are managed by women, even in the most volatile markets.

Or the bosses

There are two basic styles of portfolio management: the "superstar" approach and the "committee" approach. I would rather invest with a superstar—a single manager genius. I find it impossible to believe that a basketball, football, or other athletic team could function if managed by four or five different leaders, each with their own brand of management style and differing strategies and opinions.

The committee approach may proceed more cautiously and provide a watered-down performance. If you pay management fees, you should receive a better return than the market in general. Indexes require no management fees and reflect what happened to a broad number of stocks or bonds. Fund management should be able to improve on that record.

In a family way

A mutual fund family consists of many individual mutual funds pulled together under one general operating roof. Does big mean better?

You know that the best CD in town is usually not found at the lending institutions with the lowest interest rates on new car loans. The lowest home mortgage rate is probably available at yet a third institution. Mutual funds operate in a similar fashion—that's why they advertise so heavily to get you into anything, even a no-cost money market. Once you're "inside the store," they can show you other attractive purchases.

Today some mutual fund families are monoliths. Consolidation, to a point, offers lower overhead costs and other economies of scale to the small investor. But size may have little to do with the quality of the funds, the performance of the fund managers, and other factors that influence fund performance. You don't need tons of investments to choose from. You need to find one or two that will work over the long-term.

Do you visit one doctor for all your body parts? Eat at only one restaurant? Shop at one store for all your needs? Learn to select only the best funds in a family and ignore the others. With so many good mutual funds on the market today, no one fund family can have the best in *all* categories. Search for the highest quality fund from one family and look to the other families for other selections. One-stop financial shopping may be convenient, but achieving the best return on your investment capital is more important. Don't let a menu of selections satisfy your desire for quality investments.

Which way is up?

The degree of a mutual fund's volatility is measured in comparison with the stock market as a whole. This factor is called *beta*—how closely a mutual fund follows the Standard & Poor's 500 stock index as it moves up and down on a daily basis. The lower the beta number, the less the investment principal should move up and down. A higher beta means that the mutual fund moves significantly in both directions, up and down.

For example, a fund with a beta of .6 tends to move up and down only 60% as much as the S&P 500 swings. If a fund has a beta of 1.6, you can expect it to swing about 160% *more* than the S&P 500, .

Betas can be found by asking the mutual fund, the selling agent or through library publications such as Morningstar and Lipper Analytical Services.

Risk-adverse investors should invest in funds with lower betas than the stock market index and with lower risk to principal. Lump sum investing should have accumulation of wealth as its goal. Be willing to give up some potential upside to get a limited downside—protection against nasty surprises. If you gain a 20-percent profit and then give it all back during a stock market dive, you've gained nothing. You've also lost your race against inflation during the time it takes to get back to where you were, the time you can't replace, and the opportunity cost of being invested somewhere else where you could have made money, or, at least, lost less principal.

So how do you start?

Investors purchase new shares directly from the mutual fund. The share price of each mutual fund is determined by adding up all the values of the assets in the investment portfolio, subtracting the expenses and fees, and dividing by the number of shares that investors hold. This is the net asset value (NAV) or wholesale price (selling price) of each share an investor has purchased.

Prices of mutual fund shares change on a daily basis (except for shares of money market funds, which are maintained at $1 per share for accounting purposes). A mutual fund selling for $9.25 is not more or less valuable than one selling for $35.50 per share.

Funds are priced differently, depending on the value of the assets inside and the kind of investments the manager has purchased.

Mutual funds are neither sold on an exchange nor in an auction-like atmosphere like other securities. The funds continually sell new shares to the public.

When funds become too large or receive too many unpredictable influxes of investor money, a portfolio manager's job becomes increasingly difficult, sometimes impossible. When that happens, the mutual fund company may close the fund to new investors in order to maintain the integrity and management control of the fund's assets. Don't rush into a fund because you heard it is going to close. If it wasn't on your list before, why would you want it just because it's going off the merchandise shelf?

Funds must redeem (buy back) shares when an investor wants to liquidate. These funds must maintain a reasonable amount of cash for these transactions. Investigate how much cash is kept on reserve. If the investment policy is to be fully invested at all times, and there's large investor demand (panic) for liquidation, a fund manager may have to sell other securities to raise cash, no matter how depreciated they may be at the time. This can cause long-term damage. I prefer funds that keep enough cash on hold (though the return may be lower), to maintain stability in uncertain markets.

Mutual funds that are targets of investor timing newsletters should be avoided. Large redemption orders on an unpredictable basis wreak havoc on the portfolio manager's blood pressure and on the stability of the fund's assets. Spontaneous depletion of needed cash or liquid capital for buying opportunities can undermine a good portfolio managers' strategies and damage performance.

Different quotes for different folks

Pricing of mutual fund shares can be confusing because there are so many methods of collecting fees, expenses, commissions, and other distribution costs. Funds have changed a lot in the last few years on this issue. There are several areas you must research to understand potential charges and expenses for these investment vehicles.

Some mutual funds charge investors in the purchase (offering) price—an *up-front load*—while others charge a *back-load* (a contingency deferred load) which decreases over time. Some charge distribution fees, called 12b-1, on an annual basis. Some use a combination of these options when marketing their products to the public. All of theee mutual funds charge expense and management fees in addition to any other distribution costs.

Never purchase a fund because it looks cheap. When choosing a mutual fund, first select the best performers. From that list, choose the best value for your money. The cheapest and the best are rarely the same.

No-load does not mean no charges. Many no-loads also pay distribution fees to selling agents. Just because you can't see a charge won't guarantee that you won't pay one.

Large up-front charges hurt for a long time. But there are good-quality, conservative, mid-load mutual funds that are worth paying for. They'll serve you better than a fund that is cheap up front but can't pass the test of time. You want top quality at a good value, not the cheapest fund you can find.

Some automatic investment programs require that you sign a contract commitment. These are called *contractual plans* and can charge up to 50% of the first year's contributions. This is indeed excessive—I even balk at an 8.5% sales charge. Avoid contractual plans offered by companies. Even if the investments perform well, the gravity of the up-front expenses will drag down performance in the early years. You must stay in one of those programs for a long time to make up for the severe up-front charges. Always ask how the charges are calculated and search the fund prospectus for all fees and expenses which may not have been disclosed to you.

Some mutual funds have adopted a new pricing model, a dual system. Investors may either pay a sales charge when they purchase or pay a redemption fee (when they sell) and higher annual fees. I'd recommend that you pay the front load (assuming it is reasonable).

Midnight madness

Every mutual fund must provide investors with periodic statements of investments and financial condition, along with a full accounting of all expenses and management fees. So you can tell what companies or securities your mutual fund has chosen and how large a position they may hold. Many fund have definite restrictions on what percentage of assets can be invested in a specific company or subsidiary, so the asset mix can work as autonomously as possible. You can find out the top 10 holdings and their proportions by calling the mutual fund company shareholder service or by researching this information in the library.

Mutual funds provide year-end tax statements. This is quite convenient, as you can use this information to complete your tax return accurately. Many funds also provide investors with information regarding the average cost of all shares purchased, sold or reinvested back into the fund account by dividend and capital gain distributions. This is helps maintain accurate records of your mutual fund share activity through the years. Always keep at least your year-end statement reflecting all activity in that calendar year. Both you and the IRS will be glad you did.

Talk about profits

Since mutual funds cannot keep more than their expense and management fees, all profits must be passed on to investors. Mutual funds distribute these profits in the form of interest, dividends, and capital gains. Depending on the nature of the profit, the distribution will occur at various times.

Mutual funds are so flexible that you can change your automatic withdrawal check if you find you need greater income, call the fund for occasional additional funds, and even decrease the amount being sent to you if you don't need it. The basic concept is to keep as much money working for you at outstanding returns as possible.

Most mutual fund dividends are paid on a quarterly basis; bond funds are on a monthly basis (or every 28 days). Capital gains are distributed once a year and only on the profits from securities that were sold. Money market mutual funds can send monthly dividend (interest) checks every 30 days. The tax consequences of these distributions should be discussed with your tax advisor.

Most shareholders choose to re-invest their distributions back into the fund or into another fund, usually at no charge. Unless you are currently living off this income, you need future growth and will want your money to grow.

Shareholders who prefer to have their distributions sent to them will be paid directly after the payable date following each declaration of the distribution.

As you discover the world of mutual funds and realize that there are benefits which haven't been discussed in this chapter, you will understand why mutual fund investing has become so popular. With nearly 3,900 to choose from, the challenge is to sort through the ordinary to find the gold nuggets. The next section is designed to help you separate the eagles from the turkeys.

Separating the eagles from the turkeys

Some things, like wine, improve with age. Mutual fund performance charts are *not* one of those things. I put no credence in historic performance that dates back more than five years. So much has changed that those numbers are worthless in today's dynamic environment. Many funds tout 10-year performances, which may cover up large losses and mediocre gains after the crash of 1987. A 10-year period has too much bias toward the bull market of the 1980s to be of much help in how a fund really works on a year-to-year basis.

I research a fund's one-year, three-year and five-year performance records. This provides me with the best insight into the two largest stumbling blocks--the crash of '87 and the mini-crash of '89. If a fund has performed poorly during any one of those periods, it is culled from my list. Since I am always investing for a rainy day, looking for the best performances during the worst times, I need to know how a fund performs during a crisis. How it performs on the hot seat tells me a lot about how it will perform through the good times.

It's easy to make money during up markets. It's the famines I worry about. I want funds that will hold together during those down times, yet participate generously during the feasts. If you take your time and follow good fundamentals, you can find those stalwart performers.

Maximum growth, maximum risk

Maximum aggressive growth mutual funds invest primarily in small companies with big futures. The risk of loss is so great that little space is reserved here for their defense. I do not recommend them for lump sum investing, advise my clients to move out of them to safer ground, and can back up my concern with performance statistics. In a fluctuating or declining market, greater risk incurs only slightly better results than more conservative choices. Sometimes less risk actually enhances the potential for gain.

Those stock mutual funds that closely mirror the stock market indexes (the market in general) may be effective for dollar-cost-averaging. But you must siphon off your profits on an occasional basis and move to more conservative ground.

Ignore the lure of double-digit returns that send you into uncharted and dangerous waters, and stick to a conservative investment program that will allow time and quality investing to achieve your financial objectives.

Growth for a price

Growth mutual funds are considered slightly less volatile that the maximum aggressive growth category. But sometimes this part of the market suffers more from market jitters than tiny stocks of small companies. These issues tend to be more heavily traded and have greater impact in large, institutional portfolios. When these are dumped onto the market, their prices can quickly decline.

This category has too much risk for my conservative brand of money management precepts. Fewer equities (stocks) can mean less market drop in the total assets of the fund due to more bonds and a little cash. But when small investors panic, these funds must stand ready to redeem all shares investors want to sell. This can damage the portfolio for a long time.

Growth funds are popular today because they racked up such phenomenal records during the 1980s. But today is new territory, and yesterday's dynamics may never be quite the same. The funds had different securities, perhaps different money managers with different styles, and the current economic environment cannot be duplicated by historical patterns.

As our country struggles through periods of slow growth and tough financial decisions, markets will mirror investor concerns, interest rate changes, and the general psychosis that attend these conditions. Meanwhile, consumers have serious races to win and huge financial challenges to tackle. This cannot be done with speculation, forecasting and clairvoyance. Creating wealth can be achieved only through patient and conservative investment policies and the knowledge that whatever happens tomorrow, college tuition and retirement goals will still be funded.

Growth and income promises

Growth and income funds are a combination of dividend stocks with a bit of cash stored for investor redemptions, stabilization of the share price, and some defensive postures during uncertain times. These funds are designed to please investors who want income but also desire future growth. They may include utilities and other high-yielding stocks, bonds and other fixed-income instruments.

Gone are the days when mature companies were considered safe stocks. Utilities are touted as safe havens for retirees. But they can have severe setbacks when borrowed money becomes expensive, regulatory boards won't allow cost hikes because of consumer pressure, and nuclear exposure becomes libelous or is behind schedule. Expansion demands in the 1990s will also take its toll.

These funds are supposed to provide stable income for retirees and steady prices of shares. But performance returns show volatility similar to other categories of stocks. Investors are fickle, and they often invest just for high-dividend yields. If a company cuts its dividend for any reason, investors may flee, depressing the company's stock and drawing attention to the company's financial woes.

Until real earnings again motivate upward stock prices, even this category will be jumpy. Stocks and bonds don't always move in opposite directions. Sometimes they collapse at the same time. This category of mutual fund does not offer enough risk management and negatives correlation for my recommendation as a foundation for lump-sum investing.

The balancing act

Balanced mutual funds generally have multiple invest-ment objectives: (1) to provide growth (2) without undue risk to investment principal, while (3) paying out significant income. This means a portfolio mix of preferred stocks (those that pay high current dividends), bonds (which pay interest) and common stocks (utilized for future growth potential but which throw off little or no current income).

They differ from growth and income funds because bal-anced funds generally maintain a mix of 40% to 60% in both types of stocks, with the rest in bonds. This category is less aggressive, or risky, than common stock or growth and income funds, but more volatile (risky) than the equity income class of mutual funds. The percentage of equities generally defines the degree of volatility of a mutual fund's principal.

Tradition states that stocks and bonds tend to move in opposite directions, depending on market conditions such as interest rates, inflation, and the general overall health of the economy. This concept is still revered today, even though its validity in today's markets is highly questionable. Bonds can be as volatile as stocks, and neither stocks nor bonds like elevated interest-rate atmospheres. But so-called gurus con-tinue to preach this outdated dogma for buying the best of both worlds—participating in stocks when times are good, enjoy-ing the safety of bonds when stocks go south.

I vehemently advocate investing for some growth above that which fixed-income investment vehicles can provide after inflation and taxes, but balanced funds apply greater risk to capital than today's markets may reward. There isn't enough autonomy or negative correlation between the asset mix for my brand of diversification. When the whole world is falling apart, I want something solid—some bank CDs as well as some money market mutual funds—for my client's downside cushion in bad financial weather.

Some pigs are more equal than others

All mutual funds are not created equal, and most of them never hit my recommendation blotter. But the good ones—all-weather, all-purpose, seldom glorified mutual funds—have consistently created wealth on a steady basis for decades. They continue to perform well—with reduced risk to investment principal—through an efficient mix of investments that can adapt to changing economic environments.

If you inherited $1,000,000, how would you invest it? I'm sure we could agree on one thing: You would not direct it all into the same type of investment. You would separate and disperse it, diversify into many investments and into numerous types of investment categories.

It is not so simple to be highly diversified from systematic risk when you have a $10,000 investment stake. Or is it?

You could deposit part of your million dollar fortune into bank Certificates of Deposit. The yields will be low, but the principal is free from risk...except, of course, from inflation.

Next you might want some short-term U.S. Treasury bills, other U.S. agency short-term debt, even some corporate IOUs. The risk to principal would be small, but they suffer from yield despondency, and that means inflation risk.

Stocks have been the long-term winners in every credible study done during the last 50 years. Blue-chips traditionally offer less volatility (don't count on that today). You also need to outpace inflation with some of your portfolio. So part of your dollars would go into well chosen individual stocks. The risk, then, is the loss of principal—another nosedive like in 1987.

Corporate bonds have higher yields than either short-term T-bills or long-term Treasury bonds, but the risk of default is greater. Corporations have to offer investors higher yields due to higher risk on capital. So you will stick to large, stable companies with broad product diversification and lower levels of debt service (lines of bondholders) to reduce the risk of any of our bonds defaulting.

U.S. Government 30-year long bonds are defined as riskless regarding the loss of principal, but that is only if you hold them to maturity. The risk of default is nil, but each and every day the value (market price) of the bonds will go up and down, depending on interest rates. You may scoop up a few of these with your remaining capital.

Five types of investments, each with its own set of risk and reward criteria. But together they provide a cement to hold together during poor times, and to participate in good periods. How much money do you need to achieve this broad diversification?

$1,000 or $25 per month.

Welcome to the world of equity income mutual funds. They offer what I call "total return"—a return *on* your money plus an equally important return *of* your investment capital. Even these veterans flinch somewhat at stormy financial weather. But they suffer less deterioration than the exciting star sectors or stock mutual funds. These conservative bellwethers participate generously in good times, and they are the bulwark of my ideal investment portfolio. A balance of bank CDs, money market mutual funds, and conservative equity income mutual funds offer quality investment vehicles and a miniature portfolio even a millionaire could envy.

When interest rates decline, the stock portion may benefit. When interest begins to climb above 9%, stocks and current bonds will struggle. But the fixed income portion (CDs, T-Bills, and corporate bonds) increases its yield. This type of mutual fund is easy enough to understand, plods along slowly enough to feel comfortable, and is flexible enough for any long-term goals.

Mutual fund-mental mistakes

You're making a mistake if you:

1. Grab last year's best performing mutual fund.
2. Select the most popular fund or type of fund.
3. Choose the fund with the highest year-to-date (current year) returns.
4. Buy the fund with the best 10-year performance.

5. Become seduced by sector funds.
6. Concentrate on all-stock or all-bond funds.
7. Choose mutual funds for income when you really need future growth.
8. Chase after higher yields (which frequently mean greater risk).
9. Swallow the hype that any mutual fund is safe or guaranteed.
10. Purchase very large mutual funds with famous reputations.
11. Diversify by picking a variety of funds from a single fund family.
12. Trade for short-term returns, then switch to other investments.
13. Are trying to "time the market."
14. Buy through investment newsletters.
15. Buy through switching timer newsletter gurus.
16. Act on recommendations of stockbrokers or mutual fund salespeople.
17. Buy from proprietary companies who sell mostly their own in-house products.
18. Purchase new small mutual funds.
19. Follow the advice of consumer monthly personal finance magazines.
20. Do anything without investigating thoroughly and understanding a mutual fund prospectus.
21. Buy a fund without first understanding the percentage of total assets in each asset category and the top ten holdings.
22. Move into funds with investment policies that force them to be fully invested in any market (stock or bond) at all times, even in uncertain economic periods.
23. Buy without knowing the beta (volatility) and alpha (measure of specific management risk versus return) measures for the fund.

24. Believe that no-load means no charges.
25. Pick the cheapest mutual fund.
26. Pretend that back-loaded funds (with silent up-front charges) are better because you can't see the internal charges.
27. Follow the recommendations of well-meaning incompetents—family, friends, and co-workers—or self-interested salespeople.
28. Like a fund with less than a 5-year track record.
29. Believe that historic performance bears any relation to future results.
30. Fall in love with a fad market-sector fund.

Chapter 18

Tangible Assets

Oh, give me a home...

Few topics evoke as much emotion and downright patriotism as the American dream—owning your own home. Home ownership represents the single most expensive purchase most of us will ever make.

People purchase personal residential real estate for many reasons other than their belief that it is a fundamental American birthright: It provides a safe investment, price appreciation, an inflation hedge, family security, a place to raise children, status, plus tax write-offs and deductions.

In addition, everyone agrees that personal real estate is a very good investment, and few authorities ever agree on anything. You may lose all of your teeth and most of your money by retirement, they all trumpet, but no one can take your home away from you.

Homes have appreciated, especially in the '70s and '80s, by leaps and bounds. Everyone needs a hedge against inflation, and your home can build future equity and appreciation—tax deferred, maybe even tax-*free* after retirement or age 55.

Your home is an excellent source of credit. Parents can use home equity loans to fund college educations, purchase home improvements, and apply for other forms of debt and payment obligations. If the interest rate market becomes softer, one can always find a cheaper mortgage and refinance.

Your parents probably owned their own home, worked hard to keep it, and raised their families with the firm belief that real estate can build up internal savings for retirement and other future needs.

The Steak: Say goodbye to the notion that houses always beat inflation, that they are risk-free investments, and that they should be the first investment on your list. That propaganda has unraveled because it has seriously hurt many people who were counting on their home appreciation in the face of inflation to pay for retirement and other critical goals.

Most folks want a home sometime in their lives. I own a home and enjoy it immensely. But purchasing a home as a nest, not as an investment vehicle, is a different concept. Most people have cars, but few have Rolls Royces. Why? Because they cannot afford them. Many wives have winter coats, while fewer of them own minks. If you can afford a yacht, by all means, buy it. Spend every cent of your millions if you wish.

But the yachtless cannot spend, spend, spend. And it's *those* people who buy so large a home that they forego other goals such as college and retirement—there are just too few paycheck dollars left over.

What is wrong with home ownership as an investment? Let's compare buying a home to simply putting your money into a CD and see what happens.

A bank CD is backed by an agency of the federal government, the FDIC. No one backs the loss of purchase price of your home.

A CD can provide periodic income. Does your home? Most homes keep eating and eating and need to be fed more each year as they grow older and need more upkeep.

Bank CDs are easily portable if you choose to transfer or spend your interest and principal. How easy is your home to transport and turn into cash?

Practically anyone can purchase a CD—for as little as $100. I don't think it's quite as easy to buy a $100 home.

Real estate should only represent 1/3 of your total portfolio assets. If you own a $100,000 home, do you also have another $200,000 lying around in various alternative investment vehicles for good diversification? Or are you so overfunded in home mortgage payments and 30-year mortgage contracts that you can hardly fund an emergency fund, let alone maxing out a company pension and saving 10% of your annual gross income each and every year?

What about liquidity? Are you sure that you will get back every dollar you put into your home when you sell it? Just the costs of buying and selling will reduce those profits substantially. The cost of improvements and maintenance over the years must be subtracted from any final gain on the sale. (If you rent, these are the responsibility of the landlord.)

Lastly, the costs of the borrowed money over the life of a mortgage are nothing to sneeze at. There is no cost for purchasing a CD.

Your nightmare on Elm Street

Houses appreciate due to inflation pressures. In order to compete with current CD rates (as low as they seem), a home will have to double in price every 12 years *just to match the gross return on a 6% CD*. That is not going to happen in the 1990s.

The final and most emotional defense of home ownership is that if all else fails, at least no one can take away your home—unless you can't afford to continue paying the increased real estate taxes, school levy, or other bills you have to fund as part of home ownership today. Those are guaranteed to grow larger with inflation as each year passes.

Before you consider me anti-American, I am not recommending that you spend your retirement years in an appliance carton. I am, however, recommending you consider your personal home a nest, a place to raise children, a refuge, but *not* a continual monster to feed every loose dollar you can find. Buy the home you can really afford with no more than 22% of your net monthly take-home pay, and ignore the delusions that the money and real estate vendors promise.

The glory days of the 1970s are gone, and so is the surging demand which kept home prices inflating. You must implement money strategies that protect all your financial goals when you buy, improve, or sell a home.

Rental property

The Sizzle: Rental property pays for itself with faithful monthly income checks, the security that real estate offers, and an investment asset that increases in value over time. This is ideal for retirees who have more time to manage such property and need regular cash flows to supplement retirement pension checks.

The Steak: Small investors incorrectly believe that if a tenant is paying the mortgage payment, the rental property investment is successful. They claim it is "paying for itself." This is dangerous thinking. There are many additional costs to consider that might not be recovered in today's rental market.

It is more difficult to earn competitive profits in rental real estate because your own government competes with you. With carrots like VA and FHA mortgages and cheap bond issue money, most people that can scrape up a small amount of capital can purchase their own home.

With this kind of pressure on the rental market, an invisible ceiling exists. If landlords raise rents above a certain level, tenants have greater incentive to purchase their own homes at similar or even lower monthly mortgage payments. They do not care that they have been trapped into 30-year indentured servant plans. They only care about the size of their monthly mortgage versus rent payments.

Rental real estate should be considered more speculative than most investing. If the property is located in a changing neighborhood, its market value will decline. Real estate must be sold in an appropriate market for optimum prices. It is not liquid and is often less marketable than other investments.

If you sell the property before it has been fully depreciated, some of the tax benefits will have to be recaptured and reduced (refigured). Rental property is considered investment property, so all profits from rent and the eventual sale of the property are taxed as income or capital gains.

When you are a landlord you have a second job. It is possible to find that your tenants have left in the middle of the night and removed the plumbing. Renters may have children or pets that can damage the property.

In addition, you must protect yourself with ample liability insurance against suits filed by your renters or by those who may sue your renters and include you for good measure. This insurance cost reduces your profits.

Property must be kept in good and safe condition. There must be an ample maintenance slush fund. Disputes may arise regarding responsibilities and obligations of landlords or tenants. So there may be legal fees to consider.

If you own a single-family dwelling and your tenant loses his or her job and simply stops paying rent, it may take months to evict them and have the property vacant for new tenants. In the meantime, the property could be damaged or left poorly maintained. If you should lose your renter, you will not lose the costs of maintaining the property.

The Bottom Line: The glamour of owning rental property disguises many pitfalls not noticeable to the unwary investor. A total portfolio should contain approximately 33% in illiquid real estate. Considering their personal private residence, most folks are prematurely overfunded in this type of asset.

For retirees living on fixed income and few assets, it is risky to depend on the income of a fixed asset that demands certain expenses, may need greater infusions of capital, and less dependable income than CDs or mutual funds.

Rental property should be considered a supplementary investment option; its income does not determine whether you get three meals on a daily basis. It can be beneficial, but often not as lucrative a profit center as you might initially suspect. Careful analysis of actual costs versus annual cash flow is a must to accurately determine whether this type of investment is worth the extra risk, time, and management headaches.

Raw (land) deals

The Sizzle: Bare land may be the ultimate investment because no one is making any more of it, and the supply is constantly shrinking.

Bare land can house real estate developments, shopping malls, and have access to highways, so its sale price can skyrocket. The rest estate market is much less efficient than stock and bond markets, and bargains can be found by even the small investor.

Bare land costs little to keep up and has great leverage potential, because the only costs on land are annual taxes, which should be cheap for property without buildings or other structures.

The Steak: Bare land is speculation, not investing. Ordinary bare land does not produce an income, is even more illiquid than land with buildings, is less marketable than a lot with a structure, and is poor collateral for securing other loans (as owners of bare land have discovered when they went to lenders for home loans).

Bare land doesn't feed an owner, yet costs in annual real estate taxes. When the land begins to appreciate, costs do, too. Increased taxes reduce the upside potential as land becomes more valuable.

If development comes before you want to sell out, watch out for the assessments. Since you have a large section of property, you may pay a greater share of taxed assessment for improvements such as water and sewers. What buyer wants to pay you top dollar when your land has a $10,000 to $50,000 bill attached to it?

Land cannot be moved, and it is difficult to assess an area 5 or 10 years before sale. If you intend to make a reasonable profit after all costs, you must purchase cheaply. That means either large plots of land or land many years away from its top price. Time, as we know is a great risk, and the longer the holding period, the greater the risk of reduced profits.

When you need money, you can't break off a chunk for sale. Land can sit around for years without anyone wanting to buy it, whatever its price. The immovability and illiquidity of bare land is highly underestimated—perhaps because so many make so much by promoting its virtues.

The Bottom Line: If a disproportionate percentage of your total assets is tied up in land, or if you already own a home and are burdened with mortgage payments, buying land is as good an idea as throwing a bowline and anchor to a drowning person. Novices read about the spectacular profits others have made turning over land, but they seldom hear about those who went broke trying.

Land surges in value, languishes at other times, and sometimes sags in the middle like an old swayback donkey. It cannot be rushed, even though your time horizons may be. Owning bare land can be a laudable goal...*after* your other bases are covered.

Limited partnerships

The Sizzle: A partnership agreement is a combined effort by two or more people to enter into some type of business opportunity. This may be a medical practice, a law firm, or a group of investors purchasing raw land, a horse breeding farm, or a California almond grove. Partnerships are a common form of pooling assets, and many specialized businesses are organized under this type of agreement.

Limited partnerships, both public and private offerings, are organized with the express intent of creating investment opportunities. These can range in risk from oil and gas income programs and large low-income rental deals, to highly speculative natural resource development, venture capital real estate development, wireless cable or raw land.

Limited partnerships pool investor money solicited by the general partners and their agents. This pool is then managed by the expert general partners. The investors (those limited partners) receive units (shares) of partnership ownership.

The advantages are easy to understand: lucrative investment returns, tax credits, triple net leasing arrangements (the risks associated with all real estate expenses are transferred away from the partnership), immediate high cash flows to the investor, and professional management of complex business deals usually not available to small investors. A choice of diversified opportunities, from financing Hollywood movies to renting jet engines, creates exciting and fascinating prospects, and rating services such as Stanger assess critical data such as the fairness of the deal to investors and the background of the general partners and their previous business adventures.

Direct participation programs promise predictable high monthly income or the potential of significant future growth returns, partial or full sheltering from current taxation, legislature favor (such as low-income housing abatements), and limited investor liability to make these very attractive investment vehicles.

The Steak: Direct participation programs, formerly known as limited partnerships, eventually became *severely* limited partnerships and have been among the riskiest investments a small investor can choose. If you could feed it, breed it, or fly it, folks would buy it. Enticing sales pitches emphasizing high returns and minimizing the real risks led investors in the 1980s to greedily hand over investment dollars. During the sales process, they signed a lengthy document stating they were suitable investors and had read the prospectus (the large contract that is barely understandable to beginning stockbrokers) in which the word "risk" is used a lot.

These deals are called limited partnerships because they offer limited risk to the investor—risk is limited to *100%* of the original investment. That stark reality is ordinarily not highlighted in easy-to-read language in the sales literature, and the salesperson would rather not emphasize such a disturbing aspect. So the investor rarely understands they are risking *all* of their investment capital.

The salesperson receives a fat commission for bringing the investment capital to the general partners. Some front loads (up-front charges and original expenses) have been as much as 15% to 20% of the original investment.

If the partnership is successful over time, this is a win—for both the salesperson and the investor. But if the investment fares poorly, has back luck, bad timing, or isn't capitalized properly during the long holding period, then the salesperson and general partners have still made a fat profit, while the investor has taken an investment bath.

The Bottom Line: This is an attractive investment for commissioned salespeople. There is little investor liquidity or marketability, long holding periods, formidable risks that can damage a business deal over time, and hefty fees or commissions and expenses. If the partnership subsequently fails, there is little investor recourse unless improper actions can be discovered—mere mismanagement of assets is not a crime.

Nearly anyone can assemble a partnership document and solicit money from the public. Expertise cannot be guaranteed by someone's ability to create a complicated document.

This is not an appropriate investment for serious money. There is no control over the funds, little flexibility to change investment directions when desired, few escape hatches if the market turns unfavorable, and complicated business agreements with little real diversification. There are better methods of going broke.

All that glitters: Precious metals

The Sizzle: Gold is sought as an investment for many reasons. It is touted as a safe haven of value should paper currencies fail. It symbolizes wealth, stability, and power in one tangible asset. During times of heavy inflation and total economic instability, its reputation has been reinforced. It is purported to be the chosen exchange medium for oil sheiks and Arab countries. (If so, why are they so delighted to receive *our* dollars in return for *their* oil?) Many investment advisors counsel that clients should maintain 5% to 10% of their investment portfolios in gold or other precious metals (silver, platinum, etc.) at all times, regardless of current market price. Armies have marched, kingdoms have been conquered and subsequently lost, world economies have been altered, but the lure of gold has lingered.

The Steak: So much for the theory and the legend. Let's put gold to the test. During the gold rush of the 1970s, gold hit a peak above $800 per ounce and then tanked. Inflation roared on, but without gold. When the Crash of 1987 hit (I can't think of a point in time more worthy of a rush to gold), it just sat there, like a lonely wallflower at a high school dance.

What about its resilience during economic uncertainty? When war erupted in the Gulf, how did gold perform? I can't remember—that's how memorable its performance was. When the Russian coup was staged, gold became famous for 12 hours—before returning to its former price. We've witnessed about as much world instability, uncertainty, and total economic crisis one could ever expect during a single decade. Just what has to happen for gold prices to wake up?

Do you already own a portfolio asset that is bulging at the mortgage seams, one that also seems to respond (according to another investment theory we have already explored) to inflation pressures? Why, it's your home, the ultimate inflation fighter, whose armor has recently been leaking like a sieve in most parts of the country. Many folks have up to 80% of their entire net worth wrapped up in their personal real estate. How many illiquid "inflation fighters" do you need as anchors in a storm?

What happens when you buy gold? You buy retail, add assay costs, storage costs, assay charges before resale, then sell—at *wholesale* prices. Then count your profits—if any.

I believe there are less costly methods of handling world panic or standing out in a crowd. So I wouldn't play with the gold speculators, whose main employment is dealing in gold, while yours may be computer programming, auto repair, or raising a family. You may want to bow out of this exciting opportunity to part with your investment dollars and leave the speculation to those who have a better stomach lining for quick price reverses.

The Bottom Line: Purchase a lot of gold only if you need a lot of teeth filled. How much of your vital retirement dollars would you bet that tomorrow the price of gold is going up? Or down? Or that by next year you will have made a sufficient profit to offset the negative effects of inflation plus a reasonable rate of return? I'll stick to what I know moves relatively slowly, and whose composition I can understand, leaving the huge profits (and the attendant losses) to others.

The not-so-precious metals

The Sizzle: Silver, platinum and copper round out the precious and semi-precious metals family. Although gold gets most of the attention, platinum, silver, and copper are highly sought after for industrial uses. Investing in these may be lucrative, because these markets tend to be sporadic and spontaneous with large price movements, have active trading ranges when they do move, and offer a hedge against inflationary pressures. This is commonly called buying portfolio insurance, as metals are thought to hold their value during times of economic uncertainty.

They share a loose connection with their big brother gold and can be utilized for jewelry, numismatic (rare) coins, or even held in bar form. As gold tends to move, the entire precious metal market may move in sympathy. Additionally, these metals have their own unique supply and demand curves and investment opportunities.

Silver is currently priced at a 20-year low and may be poised for a move.

The Steak: Who's touting that it's "poised to move?" Mostly metal traders and vendors peddling silver, platinum and copper or their options and future contracts. You take the risk, while the vendor cashes the check for opening your account.

The hype is quick profits with little down and large leveraged potential for returns. Advisors that recommend a portion of one's assets always be hard assets pick up better commissions than by soliciting mutual funds.

Silver *is* at a 20-year low. But it may move even *lower* or barely breathe at the same level it has for the past two years, eating up time you could be creating assets elsewhere.

The Bottom Line: Leave the silver, platinum and copper for the southwestern Indians, who will turn the metal into gorgeous pieces of jewelry. These will more likely offer you greater value over the years than any play on metal you might contemplate. Save your pocket change in bottles and consider them your "precious metal portfolio."

The teddy bear edition: collectibles

The Sizzle: We can project our dreams and fantasies into our collections. They take us to faraway places we will never visit, to eras we can only read about, and closer to people whose values have passed useful and loved objects through generations.

From antique bears, beds, toys, signs, glass, china, furniture, and barbed wire to cars, Indian artifacts, books, ashtrays, Elvis souvenirs, Hollywood memoirs, figurines, dolls and statuettes, we search out our favorites. Whether with comics, sports cards, bottles, posters, or other memorabilia, we decorate our shelves, cupboards, window panes, walls, cars, closets, bodies and lives with what we lovingly call collectibles.

The Steak: Normally, you will not finance a child's college education or your retirement (unless this is your primary business) with your collection of teddy bears, porcelain or ceramic figurines, or depression glass pieces, though we occasionally read about such events in the media.

The collectible market is fickle, faddish, and frivolous. Today's poster bargain may be next year's bathroom wallpaper, while a forgotten sports hero card bought twenty years ago can come to life.

It is impossible to predict the future whims of the markets, and you must wait for demand to swing in your direction. Since old age is one criteria of antique value, how can you predict what will be desirable in fifty years?

If you are serious about collecting for investment purposes, first consider the "just for pretty" value. Buy pieces because they please you aesthetically or as entertainment, not primarily because someone predicts they will increase significantly in value over time.

Purchase an oriental or *dhurri* rug for its beauty and function in your home, not for the dollar signs in your eyes. Gather today's dolls or limited plate editions first because they will brighten your life, not because they might enhance your portfolio balances.

Most collectors never sell their collections. They show up in estate auctions, for small pittances of their real value and of their original prices. So these are wonderful things to leave to your heirs. Though your grandchildren may not fancy hauling around 1,500 seashells every time they move, some items—glassware and china, antique furniture and tools, and decorative objects—will be highly prized in your family for generations.

If your contemplated hobby entails substantial funding, re-evaluate its investment potential and become highly educated before trading your money for objects d'art. Buyer beware or, as we novice art critics are fond of saying, "You paid *what?* For *that?*"

What separates a true collectible from a garage sale throwaway? Sometimes, just perception and the sales pitch. The words "limited edition" could mean "limited to everything we can produce at top speed and get out through our distribution system."

First, there must be a limited supply of an item or object. Many of today's figurines sold as investments will increase only slightly due to the numbers that are currently being produced. Too great a supply will render an object limited as a future investment.

There must also be enough demand to engender significant trading activity. The Statue of Liberty is in extremely limited supply, but I doubt most folks would want it adorning their front yards.

Today's good bet may be tomorrow's garage sale, while what you call junk may be around the corner from fame. I get weak when I see the prices of things I threw away at age 21. At current prices, I can't afford to buy them back.

Art falls into a unique category due to a different ambience and character of the art industry. There are so many variations in quality, style, and individual artists that you should always be accompanied by an independent appraiser when looking for good pieces. The medium, the artist, the era, and the competition for a certain piece make all this arena skittish. Even the art world is currently suffering a price slump.

Art is worth principally what collectors will pay, and the recession is showing up even with the super-rich.

Here are some general rules for collecting anything, including fine art:

1. There must exist a market for enhanced trading activity, but not an *over*supply;

2. Claims of limited editions and signed pieces may not be meaningful;

3. Research any extensive buying before transferring large sums into any category;

4. Antique brokers are good at their craft (assessing value and what the market will bear); it is not easy to outsmart them for a bargain without a distress sale;

5. Be patient when adding to your collections. This should be a satisfying hobby, not an addiction;

6. Generally, you'll purchase at retail prices and sell at wholesale—those mark-ups and mark-downs will reduce any future profits;

7. If you are following one particular artist or sculptor, it is helpful if they are elderly or cough a great deal. Art and figurines can increase in price when the artist no longer is available;

8. All collectible markets are fickle—they may be active only once every twenty or thirty years;

9. You cannot save everything, so stick to those items you enjoy most and can pass on to your heirs;

10. Quality and good condition are vital to collectibles (unless you own the original Constitution). Train your eye to sort out only optimum pieces;

11. The more you know about your area, the better values you will find and the greater the satisfaction and enjoyment. Read and continue to learn from experts in your collection field;

12. Original condition and restoration is important in many items, such as antique cars or furniture;

13. Every flea market advertises antiques—be sure you are not buying garage sale merchandise instead;

14. Some pieces pass through dealers' hands many times before you discover them—and the price is marked up every time. Always be sure to weigh the price versus your best estimate of value;

15. I still remember the three items I *didn't* buy years ago. If you really want something (and can afford it or justify it), go ahead and buy it—there must be *some* holiday or occasion coming up;

16. Let your friends know what you really like so they can add to your collection at holidays and birthdays. It may seem tacky, but I would rather know what a friend wanted than to stick someone I cared about with something they tried to hide behind their potted plants;

17. Be honest with yourself (and with your spouse)— Most collections appreciate little over the years, compared with alternative intangible investments, but human beings do not live entirely by IRAs, 401ks, and KEOGHS. If your pleasure revolves around certain collectibles, spoil yourself a bit;

18. Learn how to calculate accurate annual rates of return on profits. An object purchased 24 years ago for $25 and now currently selling for $100 has garnered a 5.946% return per year (about passbook rate), not a 400% profit.

The Bottom Line: Think of your collectibles as pleasure pieces, not as stores of future value. Plan for your major goals through solid and diversified investing in more commonplace vehicles that are more flexible and not so prone to investor fads. You also need greater liquidity than most collections offer.

Museums collect because they have patrons and grants to purchase their pieces. You will have a major problem finding a patron for your retirement.

Gems

The Sizzle: Women should always try to convince men that gems are terrific investments, especially diamonds, rubies and emeralds (those are my favorites).

The Steak: Truthfully, the most powerful part of this investment is the satisfaction one gets from wearing and enjoying one's jewels through the years. Gems appreciate from inflationary pressures and can jump in value during certain periods. But, generally, they do a better job of adorning people than creating profits for retirement funding or college tuition.

If you are judiciously purchasing gems that will hold their value, find quality stones and have them simply set. Always consider the four "c's": clarity, cut, color, and carat. Buy from a reputable jeweler, and shop around before making the actual purchase.

The Bottom Line: Stuffing expensive pieces into safety deposit boxes doesn't allow anyone to honor or share their beauty. So don't purchase gems for purely investment reasons unless you are more than a novice collector.

Do not fold, bend, staple, glue, or otherwise mutilate

The Sizzle: Many of us collected stamps in our early lives. I can still remember the vivid colors of Mozambique butterflies, exotic birds and wildlife of the African states, and columns of royal heads in the Netherlands. We carefully sorted them, then licked, glued, pasted or taped them into our collection books. Through those innocent-sounding acts, had we, by accident, purchased any valuable issues, we would have destroyed any future investment appreciation.

One purchases rare stamps to hide them in vaults, away from people, water light, dust, and aging, not to spend hours fondling, admiring, trading, or tagging them for a coffee table exhibit. The lack of collecting fun, though, is overshadowed by dealers' claims that rare stamps have increased in value as much as 30% per year. Stamp companies suggest that current issues such as Christopher Columbus commemoratives or the Ronald Reagan series can offer a current investor future investment gains unavailable in traditional investment vehicles.

Even a recent Salomon Brothers brokerage survey indicates rate stamps were one of the best performing investments in the last 10 years. They outperformed the stock market and even real estate.

These types of investments fall into the "special situation" categories of one's portfolio that, we are told, should make up 5% to 10% of our total assets. Stamps are serious investment business today. Large institutional portfolio managers have even ventured into the rare stamp market.

There is a constant dwindling supply as permanent collectors take some stamps out of circulation and more are lost yearly through carelessness and other perils. Due to a limited number of stamp opportunities and increased awareness of both collector and institutional interest, how can future prices of these unique beauties go anywhere but up?

The Steak: Most folks know very little about philately (not to be confused with philandering, with which more people are on an intimate basis). The Salomon studies *do* confirm rare stamps as one of the highest performing investments during the lasts ten years. (Everyone quotes the Salomon study if it is to their benefit). Unfortunately, small investors mostly held the "not-quite-so-rare" types, which offered lower returns than most other investment formats.

Stamp brokers advertise additional investment benefits: (1) transportability; (2) privacy; (3) deferred taxation; (4) a hedge against inflation, economic uncertainty or political strife; (5) liquidity; (6) ease of storage; and (7) convenience of sale.

Stamp brokers can be like estate auction dealers. They know their craft well and charge what the existing market will bear. Why would they sell you, a novice who wouldn't know an upside-down Jenny from an upside-down milk mail, their best inventory? Stamp brokers are also shrewd collectors. If they sell you their most valuable issues they have just lost future profits for themselves.

As a small collector, you will always buy retail and sell out at wholesale. Many brokers simply don't have the readily available markets to get you in and out on a timely basis. They may get you out by buying for their own accounts, but only at their lower prices. The lack of a large and well-established trading market may mean less buying competition (a buyer's market) and fewer dollars for you (the seller) when you want (or need) to sell. There is a big difference in dumping $10,000 of IBM and calling a stamp broker for immediate liquidation.

It is not easy to assess individual stamp values. Price is so contingent on (1) stamp condition; (2) the existing supply; (3) the current glamour or favor of a specific issue and (4) the general looseness of purse strings in the economy.

The Bottom Line: Unless you are a stamp expert, avoid philately *and* philandering. Both perform poorly in down markets, and disruptions in either can cause ulcers and high blood pressure. Instead, search for more traditional and more predictable avenues in investment products.

Chapter 19

The Ways to the Means

What do IRA accounts, Simplified Employee Pension Accounts (SEPS), 401ks, Tax-Sheltered Annuities (*aka* Tax-Deferred Annuities or 403bs), KEOGHS, Uniform Gifts to Minors (UGMAs), money purchase plans, Cash or Deferred Arrangements (CODAs), Salary Reduction SEPS (SARSEPS), profit sharing plans, and Employee Stock Ownership Plans (ESOPS) have in common?

They are all tax-sheltered umbrellas, permitting some form of tax advantage to be stamped on top of an investment vehicle. The tax advantages should enhance the effectiveness of the investment option.

Tax consequences and considerations are the third leg of our investment three-legged stool. As understandable as that is, most folks mistakenly see tax planning and tax shelters as their first and most crucial objective, even if the underlying investment inside the tax shelter wrapping is mediocre or, worse yet, downright inferior.

If a conflict arises between investment return and tax advantages, choose the taxable investment over the tax shelter. For example, insurance products are sold as great tax shelters because they defer profits and minimize current taxes. But, for the most part, their returns are diluted and mediocre. An investor would often be better off in a taxable mutual fund.

Municipal bonds are heavily peddled for tax-free income. Investors should understand the increased risk that comes with these types of investments. A triple-A bond today could deteriorate tomorrow. In many cases, investors may be buying thin air, someone else's promises for future interest with little or no equity standing in case the bond defaults.

This section is dedicated to presenting a general understanding of shelters, an area of considerable confusion and misinformation. Check with your employer and the investment company for specific details on how your unique financial circumstances may benefit from the utilization of these common tax-advantaged shelters. Remember that in all cases, *the quality of the investment vehicle is more important than any tax advantage.* Consider these tax benefits only as the third and final criteria in your investment planning.

KEOGHs

The Sizzle: Defined-contribution KEOGHs can be set up by incorporated business owners or self-employed individuals to contribute 13.94% of net profits, up to a $30,000 maximum, per year. Annual contributions are fully tax-deductible, and all profits are tax-deferred until retirement, termination, death or disability.

These operate somewhat like IRA accounts with tax-deferral advantages until age 70 1/2 and withdrawals permitted after age 59 1/2. Early withdrawals are allowed if the plan is annuitized, meaning that the participant takes out annual payments per year based on life expectancy.

There are two basic types of KEOGH plans. One is a *defined-contribution plan,* which limits the percentage of contribution each year based on income. The other is a *defined-benefit plan,* a more confusing animal that must be administered at some expense. But the defined-benefit plans allow greater annual funding for an older individual who wants to contribute as much as possible into a tax-sheltered retirement plan.

Employees and the employers can contribute to their own IRAs even though they participate in a KEOGH plan. The tax-deductibility of an IRA, however, may be limited or totally disallowed depending on adjusted gross income for the year.

The Steak: KEOGHS must be offered to other employees when they become eligible. They must also not be discriminatory, although they can be set up to favor older ages, higher salaries, and longer service.

KEOGHs are more complicated than Simplified Employee Benefit (SEP) pension plans (discussed later in this chapter). Unless a significant amount of funds can be invested on an annual basis, the SEP is better—it has no administration or compliance expense, and the monitoring is simple. A clerical employee or accounts person can handle SEP requirements, while a KEOGH may need special attention with a higher price tag, often much higher.

KEOGHS may be more susceptible to IRS probing than simpler pension plans. IRS rules change and changes may not be grandfathered in with allowances for those already regulating their plans by old sets of rules. Some practitioners are abandoning KEOGH plans and starting profit-sharing or other pension programs.

The Bottom Line: You can pack away a lot of money in a defined-benefit KEOGH on an annual basis if you are near retirement and have a large annual income, while the defined-contribution KEOGH that allows a certain percentage of net profit to be invested may be more beneficial to a younger person.

Many professionals are so busy creating incomes that they pass off the investment decisions in a KEOGH to a third party. This is a terrible mistake. To keep a KEOGH or other pension plan active, flexible and simple, purchase packaged mutual funds and add some good quality stocks on an occasional basis. With a combination of bank CDs, mutual funds, and a small stock portfolio, the total return can be easily calculated, assets can be managed with little time and trouble, and over-all returns won't be reduced by pricey companies who sell you status and sophistication, when they should be concentrating on old-fashioned fundamentals.

KEOGHS may be contributed to until April 15 of the following tax year. Adequate contributions must be made on a quarterly basis. However, an initial KEOGH must be set up by December 31 of the year in which it is supposed to start. This is different from an IRA or SEP account.

The specifics of either a defined-contribution or defined-benefit KEOGH are too complicated to be totally understood here. Expert advice should be sought from competent people in this field.

Tax-deferred annuities (tax-sheltered annuities or 403bs)

The Sizzle: A TDA, TSA, or 403(b)(7)—its IRC Code Listing—is a retirement tax shelter designed specifically for employees of public educational institutions, and certain nonprofit, tax-exempt organizations. It allows the employee to have tax-deductible contributions. Not only can you reduce your current income taxes, but the money in a 403b account is totally tax-sheltered from federal income taxes until retirement or withdrawal. (Do not confuse this plan with private tax-deferred insurance products anyone can purchase).

There may be multiple investment vehicles to choose from, and TDAs have retirement plan portability. If you change employers, you may take your 403b plan investment with you, completing either a 403b rollover to a new nonprofit employer's 403b or to an IRA rollover. In either case, the plan's assets remain tax deferred

At retirement, you can defer taxes on a lump sum distribution (withdrawal) by moving your plan into an IRA rollover tax shelter until age 70 1/2. You then must withdraw annual minimum payments, according to life expectancy at that time.

TDAs have an attractive loan provision that allows access to your funds prior to retirement. The loan maximum is 50% of your account balance or $50,000, whichever is less, for any hardship reason. Loans must be repaid in periodic equal payments over a maximum of five (5) years. The loan principal and interest are reinvested back into your account.

You determine how much of your salary you desire to contribute (within certain limits) and how often you want to set aside funds. By signing a salary reduction agreement with your employer, the funds will be automatically deducted from your gross salary paycheck and contributed to your TDA investment company.

Should you die before receiving your distributions in full after retirement, you may name a beneficiary to transfer the account outside of probate.

The Steak: You may only receive your TDA account on retirement, death, disability, or employment termination. There are hardship provisions for loans, but they can be changed by Congress at any time and probably will. Don't depend on easy access to your funds in the future. This is no place to invest a college tuition fund or savings for a new home, car, or boat.

The most disappointing fact is that the insurance industry has cornered this market. They are great marketers and make attractive employee presentations. If you contribute to a TDA, you have a built-in tax shelter from the tax benefits available in the plan. This is a silver bullet. Don't add an additional insurance middleman by purchasing your investment through an insurance company. Insurance commissions are much more lucrative than mutual funds offer, and every dollar which goes into some else's pocket takes away a seed investment dollar in your nest egg. Due to the magic of compounding, you are giving away the future value of lots of retirement dollars you will need.

The Bottom Line: You may choose a mutual fund or an insurance annuity, either fixed or variable. Purchasing a variable annuity just adds another layer of insurance commissions and expense and mortality charges and reduces your annual return, often significantly. It provides little in benefits—you already have a tax-deferred circumstance via the TDA, TSA, or 403b statutes.

Choose a good mutual fund for your contributions, and if your employer has only included insurance products or insurance company in-house funds, request that other carriers be allowed in the company's program. This takes no effort on their part, and payroll deductions can be sent to the mutual fund of your choice.

This is a hotly contested market and a lucrative one for the insurance companies, so expect some resistance and perhaps some manipulation to coerce you to remain in their products. Avoid the best salespeople. Demand the best investments.

The SEP-IRA

If you are self-employed or own a small business, a retirement plan can offer significant tax advantages as well as critical retirement funding. But the associated expense and administration of such a program may render it impossible.

The Sizzle: Whether incorporated or a sole proprietorship (an individual in business to make a profit), a SEP is a tax advantage for both the owner and the employees.

A SEP is an expanded version of the Individual Retirement Account (IRA) for self-employed folks, business owners and their employees. The employer can make tax-deductible SEP contributions into separate accounts established for him or herself and each eligible employee. Earning on all contributions are tax-deferred until withdrawal. The employer can deduct the contributions as a business expense.

Employers can contribute up to 15% of a plan participant's annual compensation, to a maximum of $30,000 per participant per year. These contributions can be changed or even skipped from year to year, as long as employees are treated equally (no discrimination).

There are no time-consuming annual reports to the IRS or the Department of Labor. Unlike many qualified retirement plans, the only outside costs associated with a SEP normally are the small investment custodial charges, say $10 per year, for clerical and IRS reporting. Because there are no annual reporting requirements, employers save administration and accounting expenses. The underlying investment company provides individual statements to all employees to relieve the employer of such clerical work.

SEPs can be set up each year as late as April 15 of the following year and still qualify for the prior year's contribution. "Eligible employees" include those who have worked for the employer three out of the latest five years, have reached the age of 21, and have earned at least $363 (raised each year for inflation) from that employer during the calendar or fiscal year. All part-time employees satisfying that criteria are considered eligible to participate.

Because employer contributions are tax-deductible as business expenses, a SEP can mean substantial tax benefits. The tax-deferred status of all compounding means a larger retirement account in the future. The employer can offer employees a variety of mutual funds inside the tax shelter. They make great investments inside the compounding power of the SEP-IRA tax shelter.

The Steak: SEP withdrawals are subject to a 10% penalty if withdrawn (different from moving it) before age 59 1/2, unless the withdrawals are due to death, permanent disability, or an annuity (equal annual payments based on the person's life expectancy). Withdrawals must begin no later than age 70 1/2. All withdrawals are taxable as ordinary income.

An employer may not use a SEP if they offer other qualified retirement plans such as 401ks, thrifts, profit sharing, or 403bs. If the employer wishes to integrate the plan for Social Security, has maintained a defined benefit plan for themselves or for the employees, or uses the services of leased employees, a SEP cannot be used.

If the employer with additional employees intends to set up a retirement plan which favors age and/or length of service or is skewed toward the employer-owner's benefit, the SEP plan may not be the most beneficial option.

The Bottom Line: The SEP is a commonly used, easily monitored, loosely formulated, flexible employer-employee pension plan for small business or self-employed individuals who do not want loads of regulations, compliance and administration. If the number of employees is small, the employer has a significant percentage of assets flowing to his or her own account.

Accounting procedures are simple, employees have a choice of investment options, and all contributions and profits are tax-deductible and tax-deferred.

If the SEP assets are withdrawn before age 59 1/2, causing a 10% penalty plus income taxes in the year the money is taken out, the penalty may be minimized or erased due to the length of time the money has compounded and the expansive effect of the tax deduction and the tax deferral advantages.

This is an excellent opportunity to shelter self-employed profits and set up a retirement plan without the hassles generally accompanying such endeavors. A mutual fund is a natural for the underlying investment vehicle. A one-page document signed by the employer and a one-page application signed by the employee(s) establishes a SEP.

ESOPS

The Sizzle: ESOPS are a loose variety of stock employee benefits, but generally they offer benefits in the form of free, reduced-price, or future options to purchase company stock. Owning a piece of the company you work for may motivate you and other employees to work harder, find more cost-effective methods of producing and distributing your product, and may increase your total compensation in the form of an investment which is not currently taxed.

Stock options are cheaper than salary as employee compensation, and the employee would often prefer a non-taxed benefit to earning a higher (and taxable) salary anyway. Many companies have earned huge profits for their employees because the stock performed so well over the years. If the stock option is open-ended (the employee can purchase it at any time until retirement at a pre-determined price), this could be an additional retirement investment at a bargain price.

The Steak: Companies that nurture their employees from first date of hiring on through retirement are rare today. If a company can improve its bottom line by flying south with the Canadian geese one winter, it just might. Most employees are concerned that their companies will be there in *five* years, let alone at retirement.

If your company pension is at risk due to the fact that time is a risk on all investments (including pensions), why increase the chance of loss of *more* retirement assets by purchasing stock options in the same company?

The Bottom Line: Employees are often emotionally attached to their companies, and they see opportunities in risky investments and ignore glaring risks they could avoid. Systematic risk, the chance that holding something you bought too much of will go down, can be avoided. You are probably not increasing the opportunity for return as much as you are enhancing your risk of loss by directing such a large percentage of your investable income into one company.

Diversify even in your company pension options. You may be giving up a high-flier, but you won't be risking buying a dog with your serious retirement money. If your company flops before retirement time, what condition will the stock price be in? If you are lucky, it will be in intensive care with you in the waiting room praying for a miraculous recovery, wishing you had been less greedy.

SARSEP

The Sizzle: Salary Reduction Simplified Employment Pension Plans (SARSEPS) are reserved for employers with 25 or fewer employees. Employees request a salary reduction, and contributions to the SARSEP are not included in their gross salary. And, all growth is tax-deferred until retirement.

If you are a for-profit employer, at least 50% of eligible employees must decide to contribute. Contributions of 15% of gross are generally permitted, up to a maximum of $8,475 for 1991 (indexed upward each year for inflation).

Company owners, officers, and certain highly-paid employees cannot contribute more than 125% of the average percentage of pay other employees contribute to the SARSEP through salary reduction.

A company can have both an employer-funded SEP and a SARSEP. However, the total for both plan contributions cannot be more than 15% of pay or $30,000 in any given year.

The Steak: SARSEPS are hybrids of the basic SEP pension plan for small businesses. An employer pays no Social Security or unemployment taxes on SEP contributions for employees, but employers do pay Social Security and unemployment taxes on their employees' pre-tax contributions in a SARSEP.

Tax consequences are treated like IRA accounts, and withdrawals are available after 59 1/2 without penalty. Withdrawals must start after age 70 1/2, based on life expectancy tables at that time. Early withdrawals are allowed but are taxed and subject to a 10% penalty on both the original contribution and all profits withdrawn.

The Bottom Line: SARSEPS are more confusing tax animals with greater discrimination, employee participation, and compliance requirements. That translates into greater confusion. A SARSEP loses some flexibility of its prototype, the SEP.

The SARSEP allows upper management or the employer to direct a greater percentage of the pension contributions to themselves because this plan can be integrated with Social Security (skewed to favor highly-compensated employees). But the penalties for mistakes may not be worth the larger contribution to upper management.

Look at both sides of this coin before deciding which option to choose. Tax law tends to become more complicated over time. Each of these plans may be adapted by Congress in the future. I would choose KISS (Keep it simple, stupid) and in most circumstances, the SEP.

401k

The Sizzle: Tax-deductible contributions, matching employer contributions, all profits tax-deferred until retirement, the portability upon termination to move to another employer plan, a choice of investment vehicles, and tax-favored status at retirement through an IRA rollover. What more could you ask for from a retirement vehicle? Today you can even find some 401ks that will let you borrow from your funds for hardship circumstances.

This is a powerful voluntary employee plan and one that is gaining greater popularity among corporations. Any employee who has completed one year of service, 1,000 hours of work, and is 21 years of age may be eligible to participate. A combination of employee and employer money can be deposited to a maximum of 15% of the employee's compensation (up to $8,475 for 1991).

Investment vehicles such as Guaranteed Investment Contracts, insurance annuities (fixed and variable), company stock, various mutual funds, and money market accounts can be utilized. The employee's deposits are 100% vested and can be transferred to an individual IRA account at the end of employment anytime. The employer's contribution may be set up on a vesting schedule, depending on the specific plan.

The employee's salary deferrals are deposited into chosen funding vehicles. The deferred funds do not appear on the employee W-2 form because these are pre-tax contributions.

At termination or retirement, the employee can rollover the qualified money into an IRA account with no current tax consequences. Other options include taking the lump sum and paying taxes before age 59 1/2. After age 59 1/2 there is no early withdrawal penalty.

The Steak: Employees usually grab first for the tax benefits and choose investment vehicles without much thought. You may be maxing your 401k contribution and your employer may be matching your max. But if your pension plan is full of hidden charges, expenses, and life insurance costs, you may do better outside the 401k, despite its tax shelter assistance.

If your option is company stock, take another look before jumping into the same corporation that your retirement pension is riding on years from now. Are you increasing your returns or merely enhancing the risk at retirement? You could be without a pension *and* the stock option money.

401ks commonly offer Guaranteed Investment Contracts (GICs) issued by one or more companies from the industry struggling for financial footing. You may even see a higher return and believe this was the safe option. Think again.

If you move to another employer, consider an IRA rollover and work your money yourself until retirement. You will have better control and may diversify it better. Don't put all of your 401k rollover into any one type of investment vehicle, no matter how beneficial it sounds. Large pension lump sums should be diversified into several baskets.

If you have a choice of rolling over your 401k lump sum plan into your new employer plan, reconsider. Currently it is in your hands, under your control. Giving it to some new stranger whom you have never met will not guarantee an expert manager. For temporary storage, put it into a 60-day bank CD under an IRA rollover and get a financial education to learn how to build your own portfolio.

401ks are cheaper for corporations than defined benefit plans where retirement benefits are guaranteed by the company (which shoulders the investment risk and is obligated to fund so much of your salary at retirement). As these benefits have become harder to achieve, companies have switched to plans they can fund more comfortably, where they guarantee the contributions, not the ultimate benefits. The employee makes the investment choices, which leaves the employer off the hook if the employee's investment turns sour and precious retirement funds are lost or mismanaged.

The Bottom Line: I value control of money above most other benefits, even tax savings. Whenever possible, use your 401k. But if the investment vehicle is inferior (and you have complained about changing it), then consider funding less of your 401k and more of another retirement vehicle, such as your IRA account, even though the contribution may not be tax-deductible.

Chapter 20

So Where *Do* You Put Your Money?

The following investment portfolios are provided for instructional and educational purposes only. Every small investor will have a unique and individual set of circumstances, and these models are not intended to replace good sound financial planning practices.

Specific financial products should be included only after researching each thoroughly, especially how they function during both good and poor economic times and through varied market swings.

These asset allocation models can, however, be utilized to develop a general investment philosophy and avoid financial advisors who tell you they can effectively manage your money for high returns while minimizing risk. These portfolios were developed with risk-adverse objectives in mind and offer potential for growth over long periods of inflationary pressures. They also attempt to conserve the investment principal of the total portfolio, whether for short-term goals (three years or less), where conservation of principal must be of a higher priority, or for long-term goals, where inflation must be beaten.

No real estate investments have been included because I believe making paper plays in the real estate arena through either limited partnerships, unit investment trusts, or some other form of indirect ownership offers too great a risk to principal.

Each portfolio presented is adjusted for risk tolerance and assumes that the reader is risk adverse (the risk tolerance is low), is utilizing serious money that cannot easily be replaced, and that the investor is willing to spend a little time monitoring and managing his or her investments.

After the initial asset allocations (the general mix investment categories), the portfolio should stay in place and not be micromanaged. In other words, *don't fuss with it*. When CDs and money markets slump, the mutual fund portfolio portion should be working well.

At lofty interest rates, neither stocks nor bonds are comfortable and both will struggle for advancement. At that point, the fixed-income portion (CDs, some bonds and money market instruments) will take over and increase the overall return.

By chasing after profits someone else has already made (last year's best performer) and re-positioning your portfolio every time one asset category begins to sag, you will more likely mess it up instead of improving the overall value of the asset mix.

Once you have positioned your assets in comfortable vehicles, *leave them alone*.

Each of the investment allocations has the following benefits:

1. Simplicity—You can understand each plain vanilla type of investment;

2. Control—You can watch your money closely with mutual funds and CDs deposited in your neighborhood bank;

3. Accessibility—All these investment categories can be immediately pulled out in a crisis situation or to change investment options;

4. Diversified risk—Each type of investment has a different list of risks; these combined together can offer lower total investment volatility and the opportunity to outpace inflation;

5. Old-fashioned, common-sense money management—Once this portfolio has been assembled, leave it alone. The greatest mistake investors with larger assets can make is to mess up the beauty

and value of a quality diversified asset mix. Let the magic of compounding work.

A beginning investment portfolio

Our hypothetical family:

Salary: $35,000 family income per year
Children: Two—ages 5 and 7
Job security: Good
Health: Good
Total amount of consumer debt: less than 20% of take home pay (not counting home)
No credit card debt
$25,000 in available investment funds

Short-term assets

$5,000 (lump sum): A money market mutual fund which invests only in U.S. Government and agency securities.

Living expenses: An interest-bearing checking account with free check-writing service if a minimum balance of $500 or $1,000 is kept.

Long-term assets

$2,000* per year in an IRA: Using an equity income mutual fund—spouse should also contribute if sufficient discretionary income is available. Make annual IRA contribution whether tax deductible or not.

*$2,250 if only one spouse works; $4,000 if both are working.

$100/month: Into a growth or common stock mutual fund with UGMA tax shelter label for 7-year-old's college funding.

$75/month: Into a growth or common stock mutual fund with UGMA tax shelter label for 5-year-old's college funding (less money is needed because there is more time for the investment funds to compound).

$1,000 - $2,000/year: Into a 401k, 403b (Tax Deferred Annuity) plan, utilizing a greater or lesser percentage depending on the quality of investment vehicle options.

$10,000 lump sum: In a conservative equity income mutual fund which in turn invests in bank CDs, money market instruments, mature stock companies, corporate bonds of high investment quality, and U.S. long 30-year bonds. This mix softens blows to principal while providing potential for growth to outpace inflation.

$5,000 lump sum: Into a heavily diversified global mutual fund with good track record and consistency. Avoid those that invest heavily in a few countries or which have large positions in Europe. Play themes and wide diversification strategy. Select global rather than international funds which cannot invest at home when world markets turn sour and are more susceptible to currency fluctuations.

A take-off young investment portfolio

Our hypothetical family:

Salary: $50,000 family income per year
Children: Two—ages 14 and 16
Job security: Good
Health: Good
Total amount of consumer debt: less than 20% of take home pay (not counting home)
No credit card debt
$50,000 in available investment funds

Short-term assets

$5,000: Money market mutual fund that invests in U.S. Government Treasury bills and agencies only.

Living expenses: Interest-paying checking account with free check-writing on minimum balance of $500 or $1,000.

Long-term assets

$30,000: Lump sum UGMA (Uniform Gift to Minor Act) tax shelter mostly in bank CDs for older child's college funding due to limited time horizon. Two-year goals are considered short-term money and too little time makes even conservative mutual funds too risky.

$15,000: Lump sum UGMA in conservative equity income mutual fund due to sufficient time horizon to fund second child's college.

$300/month: UGMA titled growth or common stock mutual fund on a monthly systematic basis to offset current insufficient lump sum capital for younger child's college tuition.

$0: No individual stock or bond issues unless there is a larger investment pool to draw on and to diversify risk with

0 - $3,000/year: Continue employer retirement plans only if sufficient assets for college funding are available.

$2,000: Continue IRA account contributions in a mutual fund whether they are tax deductible or not, but only if sufficient college tuition dollars are being invested and projections of college costs will be met. If not enough discretionary assets are available, reduce retirement funding (and employer-based retirement voluntary plans) and concentrate on the college years at this point.

A growing investment portfolio (no college-funding requirement)

Salary: $50,000 family income per year
Children: None
Job security: Good
Health: Good
Total amount of consumer debt: less than 20% of take home pay (not counting home)
No credit card debt
$125,000 in available investment funds

Short-term assets

$25,000: One or two money market mutual funds that invest only in U.S. Government securities and agencies (with check-writing privileges).

Living expenses: Interest-bearing checking account with no charge for checks with $500 or $1,000 minimum balance.

Long-term assets

$30,000: Two FDIC insured Certificates of Deposit ($15,000 + $15,000) in separate lending institutions. Savings & Loans generally offer higher interest and both S&Ls and commercial banks are insured by the FDIC.

$10,000: Money market mutual fund investing only in Government and agency securities with check-writing privileges.

$50,000: One or two equity income mutual funds that invest in bank CDs, money markets, mature stock companies, corporate bonds, and U.S. Government bonds.

$10,000: Global mutual fund with heavy diversification in many countries, no large positions in any specific country, and investing in themes such as transportation, health care, or technology.

$2,000/year: Make annual IRA account contribution into a conservative equity income mutual fund or global fund (up to 10% of total portfolio) whether the tax deduction exists or not.

$1,500 - $3,000 a year: Supplementary voluntary employer retirement plan, depending on the quality and performance of the underlying investment options. Do not overfund your 401k—IRAs may be more accessible in the future and you may gain better investment vehicles in your IRA by choosing quality mutual funds.

A mature investment portfolio

Salary: Retirement pension and/or Social Security
Children: Grown
Job security: Retired
Health: Good
Total amount of consumer debt: Minimal
No credit card debt
$500,000 to $1,000,000 in available investment funds

Short-term assets

10%: Various money market mutual funds investing only in U.S. Government securities and agencies with check-writing privileges requested for instant liquidity and accessibility.

30%: Various bank Certificates of Deposit timed to mature at different intervals to straddle interest rates and reduce re-investment risk of all funds at any specific time.

40%: Equity income and U.S. Government short-term bond funds with emphasis on total return and conservation of principal and not on yield at the cost of deterioration of investment capital.

10%: Global mutual fund that diversifies heavily through small positions in many countries and can also invest in domestic (U.S.) securities when foreign markets are uncertain.

10%: Individual stock and bond issues

Avoid insurance policies, insurance fixed or variable annuities, or special types of investments such as CMOs, GNMAs, sector mutual funds or muni bonds. They also increase risk of capital, unnecessary with this amount of investment capital. Do not grab for tax-deferred or tax-exempt investments

What to do with $25 a month

There's no doubt that one of the best ways to save and accumulate funding for long-term financial goals is to compound your money as long as possible, letting the magic of compound interest do most of the work. But with only $25 or $50 per month to work with, what progress can be made? What can be accomplished with only $25 per month?

1. *Isolate your credit cards,* pay off every one of them if you have sufficient funds, or pay off the highest interest rate credit cards with whatever lump sum money you may be thinking of investing.

If there is remaining credit card debt, list all balances, the monthly payments, the annual percentage rates, and the total balances due. Pay minimums on all balances except the card charging the highest interest. It doesn't matter how much you owe to any one company. Pay extra monthly payments on that card balance. When the highest interest card has been eradicated, start on the next highest one and continue paying only monthly minimums on the remainder cards.

With this strategy you will most effectively wipe away what you can with a beginning lump sum payment and then pay off remaining cards with extra monthly money focused directly toward this project. No long-term investing is recommended until this short-term goal is achieved.

2. *Start an emergency fund.* Your emergency fund is just as important as getting out of consumer debt. You originally got over your head into debt because you didn't have the cash on hand and life didn't work as neatly as you expected. Emergencies will always lurk, and Murphy's Law usually applies when times are critical (if anything can go wrong, it will). A credit union, savings account, or competitive interest-bearing checking account is appropriate.

Start your emergency fund with your new lump sum before working on longer-term investment objectives. This stash of money, your rainy day fund, will be your financial cushion and give you confidence to start on other financial goals. How much should you have close by for emergencies? Planners tend to recommend about six (6) months' net salary in case of a short-term disability, loss of a job, or other short-term blocks in the pathway to financial success. But for many folks, that requirement would take forever. So make your back-up a comfortable amount, depending on your job security, how long before your next financial goal creeps up on you, and what other resources you may have to depend on in a crisis.

3. *Start an IRA account.* Even $25 per month worked carefully in a good quality mutual fund over many years can turn into a significant nest egg. Although you can contribute as much as $2,000 per year to an IRA if you have earned income, most mutual funds will accept as little as $25 on a monthly basis through automatic bank deduction.

The younger you are, the cheaper the cost of amassing the extra million dollars or so that you will need by the time you retire. You won't live like a king or queen because inflation will have shrunk the purchasing power by a significant amount. So making an extra million during your working life is not an option, it is a *must*. You must allow the magic of compound interest to start as early as possible.

Contribute to your IRA even if it is not tax-deductible. The tax write-off is nice, but the real value of the IRA account is the tax deferral over the many years that Uncle Sam can't touch your profits. Make every attempt to contribute whatever you can each year.

4. *Start a 401k employer plan.* These are supplementary pension retirement plans which employees can voluntarily elect to participate in. All contributions are tax-deductible (they come right off your annual gross income), employers often match your contributions, all contributions by you and your employer compound tax-deferred (not taxed until withdrawal), and there are other favorable tax advantages in a 401k.

Don't contribute money that you may need before retirement, as tax laws could change and you may not be able to withdraw your funds later when you need the money for other reasons. But it's an excellent option for putting small retirement payments to work on a monthly systematic basis.

If you are already involved in a 401k, review your current plan to see if it can be improved. Salespeople sell these plans to employers as programs. They explain little besides the tax advantages. This usually is enough to make the sale. You need greater information to decide where to put your hard-earned money.

5. *Start a tax-deferred annuity.* A tax-sheltered annuity, sometimes called a tax-deferred annuity or a 403b, is a voluntary supplementary plan for employees of nonprofit organizations such as schools, hospitals, or other tax-exempt public service organizations. Contributions are tax-deductible (come off your gross), profits are tax-deferred (not taxed until retirement), and if your institution allows, you can have the best quality mutual funds available if you talk to your benefit department.

If your nonprofit company does not already have a 403b, ask them to provide the option. It costs the company nothing. Then make sure they pick good quality mutual funds instead of insurance products for the most direct investment power.

6. *Begin a college fund.* The ideal time to start college investing is the day your baby is born. $25 per month in a growth or common stock mutual fund over an 18-year period should net approximately $25,000 in college tuition dollars. $50 per month will provide about $50,000 for an education.

The cost of a 4-year state school education eighteen years from now will be between $100,000 and $125,000, depending on the rate of inflation. So even $50 per month will leave you barely halfway there. But it will be much easier to get to the finish line and provide your child with that education if you start early and have a substantial sum when the school sends its invitation to your child.

Through a Uniform Gift to Minor Account (UGMA), you can legally gift the money to your child, remain the custodian to direct the investment until the child's age of majority, and have significant tax advantages to boot.

7. *Start saving a down payment for your home.* Many folks buy too much home with too little down and spend most of their lives paying enormous interest payments to keep it, while foregoing other goals because the house became such a money pit. You should buy your home only after you have saved 20% for the downpayment and can afford a 15-year or 20-year mortgage with house payments, real estate taxes, and homeowner insurance costs no greater than 22% of your monthly take-home pay.

If you have the patience to save before you get in over your head, you will be in a much better financial position to have the other financial goals you seek. $25 per month in a mutual fund for a 5-year period should net you about $2,060 at an annual 12% return. Over a 10-year period, $25 per month should produce about $5,808, disregarding taxes. By adding even more when you can, you can painlessly develop your house fund.

8. *Start a vacation fund.* Instead of borrowing on credit cards for that annual fling and spending the next year paying the money back (plus interest) just in time to get back into debt for the *next* cruise or European jaunt, start a separate vacation fund through a credit union or money market and contribute toward it on a monthly systematic basis. You can monitor your progress and gain the satisfaction of knowing that you will not need to borrow on your future in order to fund today.

9. *Create your own business capital.* Many people dream of owning their own business or developing a business which they can enjoy during semi-retirement. Investing $25 on a regular monthly basis into a mutual fund for this long-term goal can accumulate your venture capital even if no one else has that kind of confidence in your business investment.

10. *Start a self-determined project fund.* There are more goals for long-term assets than I could list. Start today for your future financial goals. There will never be a cheaper time, never a better time, and never an easier time. The best time is always right now. If you waste your money, you can learn to manage it more effectively. But if you waste you time, you have spent a precious commodity that cannot be bought back.

For goals more than three years away, you can invest in many types of mutual funds in which your principal will move on a daily basis. For goals that are less than three years away, you must limit your potential investments to bank Certificates of Deposit, credit unions or money market mutual funds. Be careful not to invest in gimmicky, fad, or new products that promise higher yields or returns but may also significantly increase the underlying risk of capital. Once you see your account growing, your mercenary instinct will take over, and it will be much easier and more satisfying to continue accumulating money by working your own money for your own benefit...for a change.

Chapter 21

Special Strategies to Cover Your Ass-ets

Debt consolidation

The first three letters in "consolidation" are "C-O-N", and most offers to consolidate your loans and reduce your monthly payments should be ignored. Finance companies charge horrendous rates of interest. Avoid these unless no other living soul will give you credit for something you really need.

There is an easy formula to reveal whether you will benefit from re-financing your consumer debt. If the annual percentage rate (compounded monthly) is less than what you are now paying, you have found a lower cost for borrowed money.

Don't accept lower payments, for longer periods of time. This will just put you deeper into debt. You'll trade a short-term cash crunch for a larger long-term problem. The object of consolidation or re-financing is to pay off debt *sooner.*

Don't grab a line of credit or home equity loan solely because the lender tells you it can be written off your taxes. You may pay more total interest. It does not make good common sense to spend a dollar to save 28¢.

Each time you sign your name and commit future dollars you have not yet created, you destroy a little more of your financial future. Don't put off until tomorrow what should be funded today. You must control debt or it will control you and your financial future.

Getting out from under: Prepaying your mortgage

Once you realize you have bought your beautiful new home on the indentured servant plan, hostaged by monthly mortgage payments for most of your working life, you may seek revenge by repaying the loan principal early, thus avoiding thousands of dollars of loan interest. In the beginning years of a 30-year mortgage, your interest accounts for about 98% of your monthly payments. It will be 22.5 years before even one-half of the payment is directed to the loan principal you borrowed when you were much younger and more naive.

By prepaying your principal, you will, indeed, cut off thousands of interest dollars over a 30-year duration. There are even some companies who can sell you programs that will assist you in this goal. They usually charge a fee and may even keep your extra payments in their trust fund (while those dollars work for them) until they send your extra payments to the lending institution.

You can accomplish this benefit more effectively and without any fees as long as your lender allows prepayment of loan principal and you specifically note those extra payments be applied to the loan principal when they are sent in.

A 30-year mortgage can be reduced down to a 15 1/2-year loan by using dollars which come out of your pocket or which have already been saved through other means.

During the first year of your 30-year mortgage, make an additional $10 payment per month on the principal. Next April, when your IRS refund is mailed to you, send in $500 of it to the lender. The second year, increase the extra monthly payment from $10 to $20 per month and, again, add $500 of your IRS refund when it comes in April of the following year. The third year, increase the monthly prepayment amount to $30 per month.

Each year continue to add an extra $10 per month to prepayment funds. We are using small amounts of otherwise fritter money from your pocket that you will not miss and making them work for you.

Your 30-year mortgage can be reduced by 14 1/2 years using this simple but effective method. As you grow more financially successful, instead of increasing your status and lifestyle, you increase your mortgage prepayment by $10 more per month each year of the loan. Since the IRS refund will be at your disposal at tax time, it can also be directed into interest savings on the home loan.

This concept can save thousands of dollars in interest over the life of your mortgage loan. But before you run down to your lender with your first payment, examine why you might *not* want to use this strategy. In my planning efforts with families, I usually don't recommend this plan of action, as good as it sounds.

People tend to have common goals during their lifetime—phases of raising children and looking ahead to retirement. They may desire college educations for their children, and all of us want a comfortable retirement, Both these goals will take some sacrifice now to achieve the large future sums necessary. The time value of money concept provides powerful numbers when dollars are allowed to accumulate early, over long periods of time. The earlier you start saving, the fewer investment dollars you will need to meet your goals.

People want to purchase the American dream, their home. But by buying too much home, they have fewer dollars to direct toward their other financial objectives. If you prepay your mortgage, you will have a paid-off home in 15 years. But will there be another goal right around the financial aid corner? Probably. If there is the need for funding more than one child's college tuition, this will require even greater assets due to the short time between one child's college entrance and your younger child's tuition time.

In what shape will your college fund be? Will you have directed your monthly payments back to your lender instead of starting your college funding plans? If your college fund is insufficient, where will you find the dollars to send your children to school?

The fashion today is to borrow, usually through a home equity loan. Now you will be heavily back into debt, and your previous progress will be down the drain. You will have paid back your home loan just in time to sign up for another one.

This prepayment strategy should only be used with care and only when you have alternative funds to reach other goals. If not, it is better to continue paying that regular monthly mortgage payment, and start your college and retirement goals early so that compound interest and time can do much of the work for you.

If you have a fixed mortgage loan (and you should only buy a fixed rate on long-term debt), your monthly payment will be one of the smallest costs you will bear in 15 or 20 years. Everything else will escalate, including college costs and the price of a comfortable retirement. It will take even more dollars to reach those future goals, while you may be under-funding those plans because you are sending extra monthly payments to your lender.

If you solve one problem by creating another, you will only make the institutions richer and yourself poorer. You can't get those dollars back from the lender when you realize you should have kept those payments working for you over the years. This is part of the planning process, looking ahead to where you want to be and making sure that certain goals don't interfere with others.

Collaterizing a CD for loan purposes

Suppose you want to buy a car for $10,000. You stop at your lender's to withdraw your $10,000 CD—you're ready to pay cash for the car. Your lender discusses another option with you. If you take out your Certificate of Deposit, you will lose the future interest (at 6%) that you could make on that investment. If, instead, you used your CD as loan collateral, he would gladly loan you money for financing your car at 10%, only 4% higher than your CD is paying. A 10% personal loan minus the 6% interest from you CD equals a 4% loan, almost like stealing from your lender. Will you take that deal?

Many folks would, in a minute. After all, where else can you buy money at 4% in today's market? Let's examine what has really happened.

First, the formula for compounding the annual effective yield on your CD is probably quarterly, while the annual percentage rate of a loan at 10% is compounded monthly. So the difference will be larger than 4%.

Second, it is immediately apparent—no matter what the fractional difference—that you will borrow at a higher rate (10%) than you will work your CD (6%). So it is financially better to pay cash for the car than to finance, no matter how long the time period.

The last justification for not paying cash for the new car is that your fat $10,000 lump sum will be gone until it is built up again in the future. But since you would be pledging it as collateral, it's hostaged anyway, isn't it? According to the rules, you can't have your CD money until the full loan balance is paid off. If you don't have access to your money during the loan period, what's the use of saving it at a lower rate, then borrowing at a higher rate?

This clever strategy is typical of the banking industry. The lender keeps the time deposit on which other loans can be made, talks you into an additional loan, and now has protective custody over the time deposit for a longer time. Sometimes bankers can be lean, mean fighting machines.

The optimum strategy is to pay cash for the car, make payments you would have sent to the lender to your own account, and you will have even more money than you started with at the end of the period of the proposed loan.

The American idea of a retirement plan

I frequently advise my clients to wager one dollar when the super-lotto jackpot is huge. Then I remind them to call me—even at 2:00 a.m.—if they win. As winners, they can afford me on a 24-hour a day basis. Your pets like you for yourself. But when you have big money, you can buy nearly anything, even the undying loyalty of other human beings.

Betting large sums on any form of gambling is destructive because it avoids the necessity and reality that one must save some of their paycheck and prepare for future financial goals. Gambling addictions of any kind can create a financially dependent and emotionally paralyzed person instead of an independent thinker who pays themselves first and watches carefully over their hard-earned assets. I certainly advise tackling major financial challengers and practicing good money management strategies over rolling the dice.

But when I'm asked which of the two options you are given to receive your lottery winnings—lump sum or periodic annual payments—is more powerful, I point out the use for the time value of money concept. You must always follow the rules of your state, but here are some general guidelines.

You want to compute which payout option has more compounding power over the time period that the payments would arrive, say for ten or twenty years. We assume that in both cases the money would be prudently invested at a similar rate of return over the time period. It makes no difference in this part of the problem whether you would invest it all, buy 17 houses for your relatives, sail to Tahiti, or purchase friends. That is irrelevant. We simply want to know whether we could accumulate more money by investing the one lump sum or the structured series of payments.

Assume that you have won the right to receive a check for $1,000,000 immediately. Lucky you! However, you have the alternative option to receive payments of $150,000 per year for the next ten years. Which do you do?

If you compound the $1,000,000 received today at an assumed rate of 8% over the total 10-year period you would otherwise receive the ten payments, you would accumulate a total of $2,158,925. If you, instead, chose the annual payment schedule of $150,000 per year for ten years, and invested each annual check at the same rate of return, at the end of the 10-year period you would have accumulated $2,346,823, a greater amount than the lump sum could produce. In this example, the best mathematical decision would be to take the payments option instead of the one lump sum.

Each state's lottery is set up on a different proportion of lump sum amounts versus payment amounts. So you cannot conclude by the above example, which option would be better in all cases. You must always compare the specific figures in your state. Do not make your decision by only visualizing the problem, as this can be misleading. You must make the actual computations and then compare your answers.

There are two more wrinkles to this problem. These are the common sense judgments that must be made. The first consideration is the risk that time creates, one that most folks ignore in their financial decisions. Pretend that I owe you $1,000. Do you care if I pay it back to you today or in ten years? The obvious answer is that you would want your money now, because you could invest it for that long period of time and make it grow. If *I* could keep it for that long period, I would do the same strategy.

Disregarding the time value of money (because I will promise to pay you annual interest), can you see any other risk that time would increase? Putting it kindly, I might not be available in ten years. Therefore, my promise might be well intentioned but fail due to the fact I couldn't come back to this world to continue paying you the annual payments.

This is a very important consideration when evaluating any type of structured settlement, such as a disability claim, a personal injury litigation award, selling your home on the installment plan or, for that matter, settling for yearly lottery payments. What if the person will not (or cannot) continue to pay as specified? Sometimes I will recommend that a client take less money and request a lump sum rather than structured payments over long periods of time because the money is out of your hands and your control. Everyone knows that a bird in the hand is safer that one overhead.

You do not win the large pot of lottery money. You win either a smaller pile or an annuity with a promise to pay (specified payments) for a period of time. These payments are either paid out by insurance companies or by municipalities, such as your state. In either case, you have to decide how strong that promise to pay will remain over the length of time the payments are to be made.

Insurance companies are traveling a rough road today. And even if they are solvent today, what will happen to them in ten or twenty years? What if that insurance company disappears from the globe? If the lottery is self-funded by your state, how solvent will it be in ten or fifteen years? Suing the state because they have reneged on your payments in order to subsidize burgeoning Medicare benefits or other more vital social programs will not net you a sympathetic ear in court.

One more warning: If you choose the series of payments option over the one lump sum payment, and you die before all payments have been received, you will owe immediate taxes on the payments you have not yet received, though they will continue to come to your beneficiary year by year. This is called *constructive receipt.* Even though your beneficiary will not have received the lottery payments to pay those huge federal and state estate taxes, they are considered your property now and will be included in *your* estate at your death. The IRS will want their tax money immediately, not when your spouse actually receives the annual checks.

It is more effective and more powerful, given the additional tax considerations, to choose the series of annual payments in lieu of the single lump sum and to take very good care of yourself to outlive tax problems and enjoy a long life.

When you receive any large sum of money, temporarily deposit it in several lending institutions in short-term CDs, and start your financial education. Follow the same instructions I have outlined for suddenly single persons who will attract a conglomeration of insurance agents and financial salespeople, all knowing exactly what to do with your winnings. You have plenty of money to pay a real financial planner for some of their time to receive an objective and competent opinion. In fact, talk to and interview several.

Until your ship arrives, you need better alternatives for college and retirement funding. If you do win, you'll have more money. And if Lady Luck never smiles on you, your future won't be resting entirely on a few ping-pong ball numbers. Chance favors the prepared, but personally, I favor better odds than "chance" for funding my long-term needs.

Prenuptial agreements

Though it may sound cold to have your bride- or groom-to-be sign on the dotted line as a condition of marriage, if you have children from a prior marriage, are unsure of how you want your assets combined with your new spouse, or have other reasons to want his, hers and yours separated, a prenuptial agreement should be considered.

A prenuptial agreement is a written contract signed without coercion or duress that states which assets shall be considered separate from marital property, and which assets are to be combined as belonging to both husband and wife. Often these assets or property come from prior marriages or relationships, deceased parents, or relatives and friends with specific intentions.

This type of agreement is becoming more popular because it spells out clearly the intent of both parties and the subsequent approval of each interest party before the wedding, the traditional commingling of marital assets.

If you proceed, consult a competent attorney who is familiar with existing statutes and has sufficient experience in this area. Attempt to avoid a legal advisor who has just purchased a piece of software on which the secretary will type out the agreement. Experienced practitioners know what has worked in the court systems and which pitfalls to avoid. In this instance, experience will not be the best teacher, at least not if it results in disastrous and erroneous distribution of those assets you worked so hard to protect and direct.

Laws and state regulations change quickly. This agreement should be reviewed every few years to be sure it will still meet all conditions of case law, statute and precedence if it is tested. This relatively new area of law is not perfected, and this type of agreement may not always hold up as well as hoped. But a written contract is strong evidence of intent in a case where emotions may rule rational thinking.

401k, 11, 84, 239
    mutual funds, 182
    tax shelter, 51, 228-230
403bs, 11, 84
    tax shelters, 51, 222

Accountants, as financial advisors, 23-24
Accredited Personal Financial Specialist (APFS), 34
Alpha, mutual funds, 186
American Institute of Certified Public Accountants (AICPA), 35
Art, as investment, 213-215
Attorneys, as financial advisors, 22

Back-load, mutual funds, 189
Balanced mutual funds, 195
Bank deposit insurance, 23
Bank Money Market Demand Accounts (MMDAs), 129
Bankers, as financial advisors
Beta, mutual funds, 187
Brokerages, regulation of, 32
Budget, teaching children about, 73

Cash flow income, worksheet, 44
Cash value insurance, 28
Certificates of Deposit (CDs), 85, 100, 126, 127, 130, 150
    collaterizing for loan, 246
    not for retirement, 132
    rates, 128
    shopping for services, 131
Certificates,
    differences from CDs, 131
    uninsured, 131

Certified Employee Benefits Specialist (CEBS), 34
Certified Financial Planner (CFP), 33
Certified Fund Specialist (CFS), 35-36
Chartered Financial Consultant (ChFC), 35
Chartered Life Underwriter (CLU), 35
Checking accounts, children's attitudes about, 77
Child care credit, 144
Children,
    money mistakes, 72, 75
    questions about money, 80
    tax advantages, 137-145
    teach about credit cards, 78-79
    teach about inflation, 78
    teach about interest, 78
    teach to budget, 73
Christmas clubs, 132
COBRA, health benefits, 90, 91
Collateralized Mortgage Obligations (CMOs), 151ff
Collectibles, as investment, 212-215
College fund, 240
College funding, 113-121
    pre-paid tuition, 116
    worksheets, 120-121
College of Financial Planning, 34
Companions, 152
Constructive receipt, 250
Continuing Education Credits (CEUs), 35
Contractual plans, mutual funds, 190

Credit cards, 238
    questions to ask children, 80
    selecting, 133
    teaching children about, 78
Current income, 41
Custodial gifts, 139

Debt consolidation, 243
Diversification,
    importance of, 63
    long-term investing, 156
Divorce, financial planning, 90-91
Doctors, as financial advisors, 21

Emergency funds, 238
Employee Stock Ownership Plans
    (ESOPs), 219
Equity income funds, 101
    mutual funds, 197
ERISA, health benefits, 90
ESOPs, tax shelter, 226-227
Estate planning, 38
    options, 157

Fannie Maes, 151
Federal Deposit Insurance
    Corporation (FDIC), 23, 85,
    123f, 126, 129, 134
Federal Reserve, 124
FHA mortgages, 204
FICA, 142
Financial advisors,
    accountants, 23-24
    attorneys, 22
    bankers, 22-23
    criteria for selecting, 36-40
    doctors, 21
    government, 29-30
    insurance agents, 28-29
    parents, 27-28
    paying for, 40
    realtors, 25
    stockbrokers, 25-27
Financial planner, definition of, 31
    paying for, 40

Freddie Macs, 151
FSLIC, 23
Futures, long-term investing, 166-
    167

Gems, as investment, 216
Get Rich Slow, 12, 28, 77, 116, 144
Get-rich-quick schemes, 53
Gift tax, 139
Gifting securities, 142
Gifts to minors, 138
Ginnie Maes, 149, 151, 182
Gold, as investment, 209-210
Government, as financial advisor,
    29-30
GRATS, 11, 145
GRITS, 11, 145
Growth and income mutual funds,
    194
Growth mutual funds, 193
Guaranteed Student (Stafford)
    Loans, 115

High yields, 65
Home equity loans, 181
Home equity, retirement, 97
Home, as investment vehicle, 201-
    203

Income tax, retirement, 94
Inflation, 61-62
    protection, long-term investing,
        156
    retirement planning, 100
    teaching children about, 78
Institute of Certified Fund
    Specialists, 35-36
Insurance,
    cash value, 28
    whole life, 28
Insurance agents, as financial
    advisors, 28-29
Insurance industry, regulation of,
    28-29
Insurance specialists, 33

Interest, teaching children about, 78
Interest-bearing checking, 153
International Association for
    Financial Planning (IAFP), 34,
    36
International Board of Standards
    and Practices for Certified
    Financial Planners (IBCFP), 34
International Foundation of
    Employee Benefit Plans, 34
Investment Act of 1940, mutual
    funds, 184
Investment
    advisors, 12
    newsletters, 14
    priorities, 49
    sales pitches, 13-20
    importance of, 51
    purchasing over phone, 68
IRAs accounts, 11, 85ff, 132, 239
    for teenagers, 144
    mutual funds, 182
    rollovers, 129
    tax shelters, 51
IRS, 49

Junk bonds, 63

KEOGHs, 182, 220-221
    defined-benefit plan, 220
    defined-contribution plan, 220
Kiddie tax, 137ff

Land, as investment, 205-206
Lender solvency, 133
Limited partnerships, 207
    advantages of, 207
    disadvantages of, 209
Liquidity, definition of, 86
Long-term goals, 41
    worksheet, 43
Long-term investing, 155-172
    futures, 166-167
    new issues, 162-163
    options, 164-165

over-the-counter stocks, 161-162
penny stocks, 163-164
playing the markets, 159
risk tolerance, 157
tax advantages, 156
treasury securities, 167-168
U.S. Savings Bonds, 168-169
Lottery, 247
LPs, 11
Lump sum distribution, pensions,
    102
LYONS, 11

Market, stocks and bonds, 173-179
Marketability, definition of, 86
Mature companies, 160
Maximum growth mutual funds,
    192
MECs, 11
MIDGETS, 11
Money Market Accounts, 129
Money market mutual funds, 129
    benefits of, 149
    definition of, 148
    tax-exempt, 150
Monthly checks, pensions, 102
Mortgage prepayment, 243-246
Municipal bonds, 219
Mutual funds, 36, 101
    alpha, 186
    automatic monthly investment,
        183
    back-load, 189
    balanced, 195
    benefits of, 181-182
    beta, 187
    contractual plans, 190
    definition of, 181
    equity income, 197
    growth and income, 194
    growth, 193
    identifying good, 192
    maximum growth, 192
    no load, 190
    portfolio manager, 185

profits, 191
prospectus, 183
size of, 185
starting out, 188
up-front loads, 189
Myths, investing, 47-56

National Association of Personal
Finance Advisors (NAPFA), 35
National Association of Securities
Dealers (NASD), 32ff
National Direct Student (Perkins)
Loans (NDSLS), 114
Net worth, worksheet, 45-46
New issues, long-term investing,
162-163
No load mutual funds, 190

Opportunity cost, definition of, 75
Options, long-term investing, 164-
165
Over-the-counter stocks, 161-162

Package banking, 131
Paper loss, definition of, 64
Parent Loans to Undergraduate
Students (PLUS), 115
Parents, as financial advisors, 27-28
Penny stocks, 163-164
Pension Benefit Guarantee
Corporation, 51
Pension maximation, 103
Pension rollovers, 84
Pensions, 102
lump sum distribution, 102
monthly checks, 102
retirement, 94-95
Planning, importance of, 59
Portfolio manager, mutual funds,
185
Portfolio, examples, 231-242
Pre-paid college tuition, 116
Precious metals, as investment, 209-
210
Prenuptial agreements, 250-251

Principal, conservation of, 93
Prospectus, 32
mutual fund, 183
Purchasing power, importance of, 93
Realtors, as financial advisors, 25
Registered Financial Planner (RFP),
36
Registered Investment Advisor, 32
Registered representatives,
stockbrokers, 25
Registry of Financial Planning
Practitioners, 34
Rental property, 204-205
Resolution Trust Corporation, 85
Retirement myths, 93-98
Retirement planning, 99-112
checklist, 105
specialists, 12
worksheets, 106-112
Risk management, 38
Risk-to-return ratio, 156
Rule of 72, 78

Salary Reduction Simplified
Employment Pension Plans, 227-228
Sales pitches,
closing, 18-20
overcoming objections, 17
tax expert, 18
Sallie Maes, 151
SARSEPs, tax shelter, 227-228
Savings and Loan, 126
problems, 123f
Savings, teaching children about, 77
Securities and Exchange
Commission (SEC), 32ff
Securities contracts,
read before signing, 67
reading the fine print, 68
Semi-precious metals, as investment,
211
SEPs, 51
IRAs, 224-226
mutual funds, 182
Sequential Pays, 152

Short-term dollars, 50
Short-term goals, 41
    worksheet, 42
Short-term money, 147-153
    definition of, 153
    money markets, 153
    safety over yield, 153
Short-term savings, college funding, 115
Single investors, 81-91
    importance of diversification, 84, 86
    keeping funds separate, 84
    personal credit history, 88
    seeking financial advice, 85
    short-term strategies, 84-85
Social Security, retirement, 94-95
Stamps, as investment, 216-218
Standard & Poor, 187
Standard deduction (1991), 142
Stockbrokers, as financial advisors, 25-27
Supplemental Loans for Students, 115
Sweep accounts, 152-153

TACS, 152
TAMRA, tax law, 49
Tax advantages, long-term investing, 156
Tax deductible, 49
Tax shelters, 219-230
    TSAs, 222
    401ks, 228-230
    403bs, 222
    ESOPs, 219, 226-227
    KEOGHs, 220
    SARSEPs, 227-228
    SEP-IRA, 224-226
    TDAs, 222

Tax-deferred annuities, 222, 240
Tax-exempt money markets, 150
Tax-favored limited partnerships, 49
Taxes, 53
TDAs, 11, 51, 222
Thrifts, 123
Total net worth, 41
Treasury bills, 148
Treasury securities, 167-168
TSAs, 11
    mutual funds, 182
    tax shelters, 51, 222

U.S. Savings Bonds, 140
    issued after 1989, 141
    long-term investing, 168-169
UGMAs, 51, 139, 182
Uniform Gift to Minors Account (UGMA), 118-119
Uniform Transfers to Minors Act (UTMA), 139
Up-front load, mutual funds, 189

VA mortgages, 204

Wharton School, 34
Whole life insurance, 28
Worksheet,
    cash flow income, 44
    college funding, 120-121
    long-term goals, 43
    net worth, 45-46
    personal financial planning, 42-46
    short-term goals, 42
Wrap accounts, long-term investing, 169-171

Z-bonds, 152